Change & Transformation in Ghana's Publicly Funded Universities
A Study of Experiences, Lessons & Opportunities

Cover illustration: 'Transform'

In this painting I have tried to capture the dynamics of change and transformation occurring in our public universities. The images and figures are portrayed in different moods and directions to represent the diverse means through which people acquire knowledge. The use of warm colours strengthens the various moods and approaches to learning and shows the associated challenges. The connection between the past, the present and the future is visualized in the linking movement of *Nkyinkyim*, a symbol of change in *ADINKRA*, the Akan philosophical signifying system. The impasto approach emphasizes the dynamic transformations in the struggle between old and new ways of seeking knowledge on Ghanaian university campuses.

Artist: **Victor Anderson Hodibert** (Ekow Anderson)

Born on 13 October 1968, Victor Anderson Hodibert obtained a Bachelor's degree in Art from the Kwame Nkrumah University of Science and Technology, Kumasi in 1994.

He was employed as a cultural worker in 1995 with the Centre for National Culture, Western Region of the National Commission on Culture, and served in various capacities relating to the development of art and culture at district, regional and national levels.

As a freelance artist, he has organized and held group and individual exhibitions and some of his works can be found in offices and private collections both in Ghana and abroad. As a sculptor, Hodibert has also participated in the design and execution of permanent mural works in some public spaces. He has also conceptualized and designed some logos including the National Festival of Arts and Culture logo for 'NAFAC 2002' and a mascot for 'Western Carnival 98' in the Sekondi-Takoradi metropolis, Ghana.

Since April 2004, he has been attached to the UNESCO Cluster Office in Accra as Programme Assistant for Culture. In addition, he is currently pursuing a Master's degree programme in African Studies at the University of Ghana, Legon.

Higher Education in Africa

All titles published in association with Partnership for Higher Education in Africa

Daniel Mkude, Brian Cooksey & Lisbeth Levey
Higher Education in Tanzania
A Case Study

Nakanyike B. Musisi
& Nansozi K. Muwanga
Makerere University in Transition 1993–2000
Opportunities & Challenges

Mouzinho Mário, Peter Fry, Lisbeth Levey
& Arlindo Chilundo
Higher Education in Mozambique
A Case Study

Nico Cloete, Pundy Pillay,
Saleem Badat & Teboho Moja
National Policy & a Regional Response
in South African Higher Education

Kilemi Mwiria, Njuguna Ng'ethe, Charles Ngome,
Douglas Ouma-Odero, Violet Wawire & Daniel Wesonga
Public & Private Universities in Kenya
New Challenges, Issues & Achievements

Charmaine Pereira
Gender in the Making of the Nigerian
University System

Takyiwaa Manuh, Sulley Gariba &
Joseph Budu
Change & Transformation in Ghana's
Publicly Funded Universities
A Study of Experiences, Lessons & Opportunities

Change & Transformation
in Ghana's Publicly Funded Universities
A Study of Experiences, Lessons & Opportunities

Takyiwaa Manuh
Director, Institute of African Studies
University of Ghana, Legon

Sulley Gariba
Director, Institute for Policy Alternatives,
Tamale

Joseph Budu
Former Deputy Registrar (Personnel)
University of Ghana, Legon

Published in association with
Partnership for Higher Education in Africa

James Currey
OXFORD

Woeli Publishing Services
ACCRA

Partnership for Higher Education in Africa
IGEMS, New York University
The Steinhardt School of Education
726 Broadway, Room 532
New York, NY 10003

Published by
James Currey Ltd   Woeli Publishing Services
73 Botley Road   P.O. Box NT 601
Oxford   Accra New Town, Ghana
OX2 0BS

with the support of the Partnership for Higher Education in Africa, an initiative of
Carnegie Corporation of New York, Ford Foundation, The John D. and Catherine T.
MacArthur Foundation and The Rockefeller Foundation. The views expressed are
those of the authors and not necessarily the foundations that funded this work.

1 2 3 4 5 11 10 09 08 07

British Library Cataloguing in Publication Data
Manuh, Takyiwaa
    Change & transformation in Ghana's publicly funded
    universities : a study of experiences, lessons &
    opportunities - (Higher education in Africa)
    1. Public universities and colleges - Ghana 2. Education,
    Higher - Ghana. 3. Educational change - Ghana
    I. Title. II. Gariba, Sulley, 1958- III. Budu, Joseph
    IV. Partnership for Higher Education in Africa
    378.6'67

ISBN 978-0-85255-171-4 Paper

Library of Congress Cataloging-in-Publication Data
is available

Typeset in 10/11 pt Monotype Photina
by Long House Publishing Services, Cumbria, UK
Printed and bound in Malaysia

Contents

List of Tables, Figures & Boxes   x
List of Acronyms   xii
Preface to the Series   xii
Acknowledgements   xv

1

Chronicling Change & Transformation
in Ghana's Universities

Chronicling Change & Transformation in Ghana's Universities   1
    Background & rationale   1
    Organization of chapters   4
    Scope & methodology   5
    Themes for the study   6
    Conceptualizing the university-society interface   7
    Education, poverty & development   10
    Universities & the challenge of knowledge production   15

2

Ghana: National Context, Socio-economic &
Political Development

Ghana: National Context, Socio-economic & Political Development   20
    Geopolitical & socio-economic background   20
    Ghana's medium-term development & poverty reduction strategy   28

3

The System of Higher Education

The System of Higher Education   31
    The institutions   32
    The establishment & growth of public universities   34
    The policy environment   37
    Government-university relations during three periods   39
    Education sector reforms   42
    Relationships among tertiary sector institutions   46
    Potential for tertiary education in national development   51
    Summing up   51

Contents

4

**Research & Knowledge Production
in Ghanaian Universities**   53
    The policy environment   57
    Research programmes in the universities   59
    University spending on knowledge production   61
    Ensuring research capacity   63
    Universities & policy engagement   70
    Quality assurance measures   72
    The role of libraries   73
    Summary   78

5

Ensuring Access with Equity   79
    Equity issues   86
    Socio-economic equity   87

6

Resource Mobilization & Management   89
    Human resource management & institutional development   89
    Financial resource mobilization & management   96

7

**The use of Information & Communication Technologies
in Teaching, Learning & Management Services**   106
    The ICT environment in Ghana   106
    ICT policies   107
    ICT structures & systems   109
    The use of ICT in libraries   114
    Co-operation & networking among Ghana's public
        university libraries   115
    Suggestions for the future   116
    Summary   116

8

Governance & Participation | 118
Democratization processes in/outside universities | 118
Autonomy & governance | 118
Governance, participation & accountability | 119
Strategic leadership | 120
Strategic planning: visions & perspectives of change | 123

9

Gender in the Institutions | 128
The policy environment & gender | 129
Female enrolment in the universities | 131
Female representation among academic & professional staff | 134
Gender & the place of women in the institutions | 136
Sexual cultures & relationships | 138
Gender in the curricula | 141
Resources for gender studies | 142

10

Challenges, Lessons & Recommendations | 144
Complexity of the reform context | 144
Growing poverty & the role of universities | 145
Universities as social & political communities | 145
Strategic leadership & drivers of change | 146
The place of private universities | 147
Challenges of integrating HIV-AIDS in university transformation | 148
Recommendations | 149
Designing change efforts | 149
Scaling-up innovations & best practices | 152
Meeting the demands of the future | 156
Managing change & transformation | 157
Conclusion | 158

APPENDIX: Institutional Profiles | 160
Kwame Nkrumah University of Science & Technology | 160
University of Cape Coast | 162
University of Education, Winneba (UEW) | 164
The University for Development Studies | 165
University of Ghana | 166

References | 170

List of Tables, Figures & Boxes

Tables

1 Macroeconomic indicators, 1983–2000: annual averages 22
2 Education targets in the GPRS, 2002–4 (%) 29
3 Enrolment in public tertiary institutions for 2003 and 2004 33
4 Staff members at the University of Ghana 42
5 KNUST recurrent budget: allocations by activities, 2001 62
6 KNUST postgraduate degrees by faculty/school and gender, 1998–2000 65
7 Library costs as a percentage of total university expenditures, 1996–2000 74
8 Applications and admissions into University of Ghana, 1997–2001 80
9 Secondary schools contributing 50 per cent or more of students to universities 81
10 Region of origin of selected students by university 83
11 Region of residence of selected students by university 83
12 UDS student enrolment by year, faculty and gender, 1993-94/2002-03 86
13 Student/academic staff ratios and norms for public universities, 2003/2004 90
14 KNUST staff by grade, March 2002 90
15 Academic staff pyramid by discipline in the public universities, 2003–04 91
16 University faculty by age group 92
17 Age profile of universities' academic staff (1998/1999) 92
18 Funding levels for universities: 1991/92–2000/2001, Ghana cedis 96
19 Recommended sources for funding increases 98
20 Major sources of funding within the education sector, 1999–2001, cedis bn 101
21 Faculty satisfaction with access to facilities (%) 110
22 Students' satisfaction with facilities (%) 110
23 Students' expectation of skills to be acquired (%) 110
24 Boys' & girls' enrolment in primary, junior and senior secondary schools, 1991–2001 132
25 KNUST staff by category and gender 135
26 UG staff by category and gender 135

Figures

1	Conceptual framework	8
2	Regional poverty profiles in Ghana	24
3	Poverty by socio-economic groups	25
4	Location of public universities in Ghana	35
5	Motivation of faculty members	93
6	Use of information technology facilities	111
7	Trends in female enrolment at UCC 1962/3–2001/2	133
8	Designing and managing change and transformation efforts	151

Boxes

1	The drift towards the market I: the emergence of private universities	48
2	The University for Development Studies: a search for difference and relevance	54
3	The drift towards the market II: market-driven courses at UCC	56

List of Acronyms

AAU	Association of African Universities
AFUF	Academic Facilities User Fees
AVU	African Virtual University
CARLIGH	Consortium of Academic and Research Libraries in Ghana
CDD	Centre for Democratic Development
CEPA	Centre for Economic Policy Analysis
CSIR	Council for Scientific and Industrial Research
CSPS	Centre for Social Policy Studies
CULD	Committee of University Librarians and Deputies
CVC	Committee of Vice-Chancellors
CVCP	Committee of Vice-Chancellors and Principals
DANIDA	Danish International Development Agency
FIDS	Faculty of Integrated Development Studies
FTE	Full-time Equivalent
FUSSAG	Federation of Universities' Senior Staff Association of Ghana
GAUA	Ghana Association of University Administrators
GETFund	Ghana Education Trust Fund
GIJ	Ghana Institute of Journalism
GILLDDNET	Ghana Interlibrary Lending and Document Delivery Network
GIMPA	Ghana Institute of Management and Public Administration
GLSS	Ghana Living Standards Survey
GPRS	Ghana Poverty Reduction Strategy
HIPC	Heavily Indebted Poor Countries
ICT	Information and Communication Technologies
IEA	Institute of Economic Affairs
IGF	Internally Generated Funds
ILL	Inter-Library Lending
ISSER	Institute of Statistical, Social and Economic Research
KNUST	Kwame Nkrumah University of Science and Technology
MOE	Ministry of Education, Science and Sports
MTEF	Medium-Term Expenditure Framework
NAB	National Accreditation Board
NABPTEX	National Board for Professional and Technician Examinations
NAFTI	National Film and Television Institute
NCHE	National Council for Higher Education
NCTE	National Council for Tertiary Education
NUGS	National Union of Ghana Students
PEF	Private Enterprise Foundation
PNDC	Provisional National Defence Council
RFUF	Residential Facilities User Fees
SACOST	School and Community Science Technology Studies
SAP	Structural Adjustment Programme
SRC	Students Representative Council

SSNIT	Social Security and National Insurance Trust
SWAp	Sector-wide Approach
TEWU	Teachers' and Educational Workers' Union
TFP	Total Factor Productivity
TUC	Trades Union Congress
UEW	University of Education, Winneba
UCC	University of Cape Coast
UDS	University for Development Studies
UG	University of Ghana
UTAG	University Teachers Association of Ghana
VCG	Vice Chancellors, Ghana
WUC	Western University College

Preface to the Series

The Partnership for Higher Education in Africa began as an affirmation of the ability of African universities to transform themselves and promote national development. We, the presidents of four US foundations – Carnegie Corporation of New York, the Ford Foundation, the John D. and Catherine T. MacArthur Foundation, and the Rockefeller Foundation – came together out of a common belief in the future of African universities. Our interest in higher education proceeds from a simple faith that an independent scholarly community supported by strong universities goes hand-in-hand with a healthy, stable democracy. Universities are vitally important to Africa's development. Their crucial activities in research, intellectual leadership, and developing successive generations of engaged citizens will nourish social, political, and economic transformation in Africa. By pooling our resources, the foundations will help advance the reform of African universities and accelerate the development of their countries.

Much of sub-Saharan Africa has suffered deep stagnation over the last two decades, and is staggering under the weight of domestic and international conflict, disease (especially the plague of HIV/AIDS), poverty, corruption, and natural disasters. Its universities – once shining lights of intellectual excitement and promise – suffered from an enormous decline in government resources for education. In the late 1990s, however, things began to change in a number of countries. Our interest was captured by the renewal and resurgence that we saw in several African nations and at their universities, brought about by stability, democratization, decentralization and economic liberalization. Within these universities a new generation of leadership has stepped forward to articulate a vision for their institutions, inspiring confidence among those who care about African higher education. The case studies found that, while the universities represented in these volumes have widely varying contexts and traditions, they are all engaged in broad reform: examining and revising their planning processes, introducing new techniques of financial management, adopting new technologies, reshaping course structures and pedagogy, and reforming practices of governance.

The higher-education studies published in this series focus on the countries that the Partnership has selected for concentration: initially Ghana, Mozambique, Nigeria, South Africa, Tanzania, and Uganda. Kenya was added in 2005. These countries were chosen because their universities were initiating positive change, developing a workable planning process, and demonstrating genuine commitment to national capacity-building, in contexts of national reform.

The studies commissioned by the Partnership were carried out under the leadership of local scholars, using a methodology that incorporates feedback from the institutions under study and involving a broad range of stakeholders.

The publication of the case studies in this series is closely in line with the major aims of the Partnership:

- generating and sharing information about African universities and higher education
- supporting universities seeking to transform themselves
- enhancing research capacity on higher education in Africa
- promoting collaboration among African researchers, academics and university administrators

The studies are the product of the foundations' support for conceptual work that generates information about African higher education and university issues. Through the case studies, the foundations hope to promote a wider recognition of the importance of universities to African development. Additional studies on Kenya and Nigeria will be published in 2007.

When the Partnership was established in 2000 we pledged $100 million in support of higher education in Africa. Working together, the foundations exceeded that goal and contributed $150 million through September 2005 to fund higher education reform efforts in the targeted countries and institutions involved. The Partnership was relaunched for a second five-year period on 16 September 2005. The relaunch represented several milestones – two additional foundations joined the Partnership – the William and Flora Hewlett Foundation and the Andrew W. Mellon Foundation. Together, the six foundations have pledged a minimum of $200 million over the next five years. And, finally, Kenya was added to the list of Partnership countries. The conceptual work supported by the individual foundations, working together in partnership towards a common vision, seeks to ensure the strengthening of institutional capacity for research on higher education in Africa and wide dissemination of African research output.

We hope that the publication of these case studies will help advance the state of knowledge about higher education in Africa and support the movement for university reform on the continent. Equally significant, the process of our involvement in the case studies has enhanced our own understanding and helped the foundations focus future efforts of the Partnership. Interest in higher education in Africa has grown since the Partnership was launched in 2000. In this way, the Partnership not only uses its own resources but also acts as a catalyst to generate the support of others, on the continent and elsewhere, for African universities as vital instruments for development. We see these case studies as a critical step in the process of regeneration and transformation.

Vartan Gregorian, President
CARNEGIE CORPORATION OF NEW YORK

Susan Berresford, President
THE FORD FOUNDATION

Jonathan Fanton, President
JOHN D. AND CATHERINE T. MACARTHUR FOUNDATION

Judith Rodin, President
ROCKEFELLER FOUNDATION

Acknowledgements

This study on Change and Transformation in Ghana's publicly funded universities is part of a series of case studies of African universities commissioned and funded by four foundations – the Carnegie Corporation of New York and the Ford, Rockefeller and MacArthur Foundations – as part of their Partnership on Higher Education in Africa. The study chronicles ongoing efforts, successes and challenges in the system of university education, research and community service in Ghana. Its overall goal is to generate increased policy and public awareness and interest about the issues and challenges of higher education in Ghana.

The study was prepared by a team comprising Professor Takyiwaa Manuh, Director of the Institute of African Studies at the University of Ghana, Legon, as team leader; Dr Sulley Gariba, a policy analyst and Director of the Institute for Policy Alternatives in Tamale, Ghana; and Mr Joseph Budu, a university administrator, who at the time of the study, was Deputy Registrar (Personnel) at the University of Ghana, Legon. Mr Christopher Agyare served as research assistant to the team. Counterpart teams of academic and senior administrative staff in all five public universities supported the study. Mr Joshua Kwesi Aikins, visiting graduate student, University of Ghana, and Ms Abena Mainoo of Swarthmore College, USA, provided invaluable support in the final editing of the manuscript for publication.

The team is grateful to the National Council for Tertiary Education (NCTE) and its Executive Secretary, Mr Paul Effah, for providing administrative co-ordination of the study, and to the steering committee, chaired by Professor George Benneh, for guidance and strategic advice. The Vice-Chancellors of the five publicly funded universities, heads of selected private universities and principals of Ghana's polytechnic institutions contributed immensely to the dialogue about broad conceptions of change and transformation and participated in various sessions organized by the study team, including the validation of the initial drafts. Members of Ghana's Parliamentary Select Committee on Education were supportive of the study and participated actively; we thank them for their interest and support. We also wish to thank the former Minister for Education, Professor Christopher Ameyaw-Ekumfi, for taking time out of his busy schedule to receive us, and for participating in a session during the case-study meeting in Accra.

We wish to thank the numerous university personnel – administrators, staff and students – and policy-makers and representatives of donor agencies concerned with higher education who participated in various ways in the study.

Finally, we wish to thank the four foundations for their generous funding and support which made the study possible. In particular, the team wishes to express its deepest appreciation to Dr Narciso Matos, Senior Programme Officer of the Carnegie Foundation, for his keen interest and assistance. We also thank case-study authors in the other African countries supported through the Partnership for generously sharing their work with us.

Takyiwaa Manuh, Sulley Gariba and Joseph Budu

1 Chronicling Change & Transformation in Ghana's Universities

Background & rationale

Since the mid-1990s, there has been renewed interest in the prospects of growth and recovery in Africa by a variety of governmental and non-governmental actors. The characterization of the continent as a 'basket case' has given way to a realization that, despite its monumental problems, there are several rays of hope, thanks to quiet, unsung efforts at building a foundation for sustained growth, prosperity and pro-poor development. Despite the constraints and challenges posed by rapidly changing social structures, declining incomes, war and conflict in several countries and the HIV/AIDS pandemic, individuals, community groups and institutions have demonstrated the capacity for incredible resilience against the many odds of daily survival. As governments in Africa have adjusted to the implications of shrinking and sometimes misapplied resources, universities have been caught up in the need to fabricate new and creative coping mechanisms to reflect changing environments. However, these preoccupations have also stunted growth and transformation in many African universities and have diminished their influence over policy choices and developments in the wider society.

In Ghana, the promise of accelerated economic growth and social transformation at independence led to the establishment of varied yet specialized human resources and institutions with science and technology as a central feature, and the teaching and learning of varied expertise in an environment of liberal studies and critical thinking as key priorities. Universities were established in part to promote this vision, both at the level of functional professionals and in the teaching of science and technology. After a decade or so of independence, this optimism was curtailed by political and economic crises characterized by sporadic changes of governments and inconsistent policies, including those of higher education. The result of all this was two decades of crisis management in Ghana's economy, institutions and universities.

Nearly 20 years of structural adjustment programming at the macro-level (1982 to 2001) have resulted in a mixed menu of reforms in the system and processes of university education. While

1

some of these may have been triggered and sustained by internal pressures within the universities themselves, others have been catalyzed by the realities of an external political economy dominated by adjustment, fiscal restraint and Ghana's recent status as a Heavily Indebted Poor Country (HIPC).[1] It is in this context of an over-arching system of national reforms that a focus on coping strategies, change and transformation of Ghana's publicly funded universities has been adopted.

Universities in Ghana have been challenged both internally by their own publics and externally by governments and communities to address these critical issues: expanding access with equity; quality and relevance; knowledge production and its application to the problems facing society; sustainable funding and resource management, all of which have called into question the roles and mission of universities in Africa. The public universities have faced competition from offshore universities (mainly religious-based plus a few secular private universities) as well as from other non-university centres of knowledge production and research. This new competition is taking place within the context of neo-liberal economic policies characterized by market-led reforms and private sector initiatives. The universities have singularly, or in concert, adopted different strategies and measures to expand enrolment, generate additional funding and review curricula and modes of operation in an attempt to respond to these challenges.

In support of such efforts, four foundations – the Carnegie Corporation of New York and the Rockefeller, MacArthur and Ford Foundations – announced the Partnership for Higher Education in Africa.

The key purpose of the study as elaborated at the consultative meeting in Nairobi in February 2001 was: 'to offer an opportunity for self-directed reflection by universities, and potentially by administrators of whole higher education systems, so they could examine their values, mission and relevance without pressure from outside sources'. This constitutes a central part of the overall objectives of a compendium of studies on university transformation in Africa[2] to:

---

[1] The Government of Ghana officially joined the HIPC Initiative in March 2001.
[2] The study on Ghana is in the series of Case Studies on Change and Transformation in African Universities. The other studies concern universities in Uganda, Tanzania, Kenya, Mozambique, South Africa and Nigeria.

- identify the causes, nature and consequences of transformation in the university and its surrounding system;
- promote a catalytic process within the university to assist strategic thinking and management on institutional development;
- reinforce and accelerate positive changes within the university;
- identify opportunities for external assistance and funding from other donors in supporting and reinforcing the transformation processes.

In addition to the above general objectives, the particular focus of the Ghana study involved an effort to:
- identify the main trends in transformation, as Ghana's universities seek to adjust to their mandate, expand access, increase their relevance and survive in a competitive market;
- analyze the critical path adopted in reforming university orientation, governance, content and impacts;
- document positive practices in such areas as expanding access and equity, seeking relevance and sustaining funding and resource management through such efforts as strategic planning, use and management of information and communication technologies (ICT), gender equity and financial sustainability measures;
- recommend strategies for scaling up best practices in educational transformation, as well as for mobilizing resources to facilitate Ghanaian universities' sustained growth and development.

The study takes as its point of departure the circumstances under which the universities' activities interface with the wider society and institutions, and the concomitant effect of that engagement in the establishment of new paradigms for teaching, research and learning. Transformation is thus seen as a dynamic and cyclical process, giving meaning and relevance to both the protagonists of the actions (the universities) and those who demand, benefit from and are affected by them (the society and economy).

Seen in this context, transformation and change in Ghana's public universities have not been altogether deliberate. Their origins, motivation and purposes have been diverse, and their feedback into the system of university education and the attendant changes fostered by these nascent transformations are still unfolding. The beginnings of these can then be characterized as innovations (cf. Ng'ethe et al.,

3

2003) – new ways of doing things under extremely difficult circumstances – in the system of tertiary education and in the socio-economic development processes of Ghana, with the potential for scaling up and expansion.

Organization of chapters

The first part of the study – Chapters 1 through 3 – sets the context within which the main themes underpinning transformation are treated. Chapter 1 starts with the background to the study, setting out study objectives, scope and methodology and the conceptual framework adopted by the study. Chapter 2 contains an analysis of the country and the socio-economic context. Chapter 3 describes the system of higher education, including a brief assessment of the universities' relationships with other institutions. It also examines government-university relations over time and their impact on the performance and prospects of the publicly funded universities.

Part two (Chapters 4 through 10) analyzes the main findings around the themes covered in the study. Chapter 4 deals with knowledge production, with a focus on university mandates and the policy context, research programmes and resources devoted to them in the universities' budgets and efforts at ensuring research capacity through an analysis of postgraduate training, the development of networks and collaborations and quality assurance measures. Chapter 5 contains an analysis of the issues surrounding access with equity, highlighting the fact that increased enrolments do not necessarily mean equal opportunity of access for different groups of people. Here, the challenges of access and equity in higher education development are examined against the evidence obtained from interviews and surveys of students and faculty. Chapter 6 highlights the issue of human and financial resource management and institutional development, and examines the variety and versatility of funding sources. The use and management of information and communication technologies in Ghana is covered in Chapter 7. In Chapter 8, issues of university governance and participation are examined in the context of leadership, institutions and systems for decision-making, including the strategic planning of change in academic and non-academic affairs. Chapter 9 presents a gendered analysis of enrolment, attitudes and practices as well as institutional manifestations of gender inequities. Chapter 10, the concluding chapter, deals with challenges and lessons to be drawn from the foregoing analysis and proposes some recommendations. We make an effort to take into account the concerns and questions raised during the partnership meeting held in Ghana in September 2002, where the study's report was presented and discussed.

Scope & methodology

In applying its conceptual framework, the study focused primarily on the publicly funded universities in Ghana, given their relatively longer periods of existence, their depth of involvement in public policy processes and their wider socio-economic linkages. In relation to the public universities, each of which has a specific focus and mandate, the study authors decided to cover all of them to varying extents, rather than to select only a few. But the focus was not merely locational; the intention was to concentrate on cross-cutting themes or innovations found across several universities. Where factors existed that contributed to change or innovation in other institutions but did not generate change in this particular instance, they were also investigated.

Counterpart teams were set up in each university to assist the research team in collecting data, conducting interviews and setting up groups for focused discussions, as well as in generating participation and a sense of ownership in the study among the universities.[3] These teams were selected in consultation with the Vice-Chancellors and consisted of an academic staff member and an administrator. They served as access points into the universities and were invaluable in providing secondary data on the institutions and in administering the data collection instruments developed by the research team.

The study also provided opportunities for interaction with other segments of the tertiary educational system, namely, the polytechnics and emerging private universities, which also present challenges and opportunities for co-operation.

[3] Counterpart teams provided basic information about the institutions from which the authors derived the information in Appendix 1. They also administered the questionnaires that the authors had designed.

The methodology for the study was highly participatory and involved six steps:

- consultations with key university personnel to develop a shared understanding of innovation and transformation;
- detailed focused group sessions with key stakeholders through an extensive field process in which qualitative data on the trends and manifestations of change and innovation were collected and analyzed;
- a questionnaire administered to students and members of the academic staff to obtain basic quantitative and some qualitative perspectives on the main issues and themes of transformation;
- review of university documents and basic statistics;
- feedback to the key stakeholders of the results and implications of the study with regard to the way forward for the universities' transformation;
- specially commissioned studies on libraries, gender and ICT.

Two consultative workshops were held in order to initiate the process and generate a sense of ownership and participation as well as to obtain a common understanding of the issues involved and to agree on the means to conduct the study. The first workshop was with Vice-Chancellors of the publicly funded universities, while the second convened principals and heads of polytechnics and private universities. Though the main units of analysis were the public universities, it was deemed useful to have an initial consultation with the heads of the private universities and the polytechnics in order to develop as broad a view as possible of the tertiary education system, as well as to identify processes of internal reform already under way in those institutions.

Themes for the study

Public universities in Ghana have responded in diverse ways to the challenges of knowledge production, access, equity, ICT, gender, the mobilization and management of resources and the governance of their institutions, often in line with developments in the larger political economy. While many of these responses have been administrative mechanisms for coping with crises, a few have been inspired by strategic concerns, thus raising their potential for transformation. With regard to the results of innovation and change, a number of themes were explored to examine the interface between university practices and their ongoing impact on the society and economy. These included:

- knowledge production, including the quality of teaching and research;
- access with equity and outreach;
- gender and institutional cultures;
- resource mobilization, human resource development and management;
- information and communication technologies;
- HIV/AIDS;
- governance and participation.

The challenges that universities in Ghana face, and their responses to cope with them, are shaped by economic, political and institutional environments undergoing considerable stress and uncertainty, as well as ongoing macroeconomic, political and institutional reforms along with the impact of policy changes thereon.

Conceptualizing the university-society interface

To a large extent, processes of transformation in universities are affected as much by internal processes within the universities themselves as they are by the national context and other economic influences affecting demand and supply conditions, which have created synergies between universities and other key institutions and firms with positive effects. Three key hypotheses have influenced the conceptual framework of the study:

- First, that the internal organization of the universities themselves – including their governance and administrative structures, policy frameworks and attention to issues of equity, environment, gender and sustainability – sets the limits to remedial change and transformation efforts.
- Second, that the way a university conceives of, and positions itself in, its research and other knowledge-production activities can

7

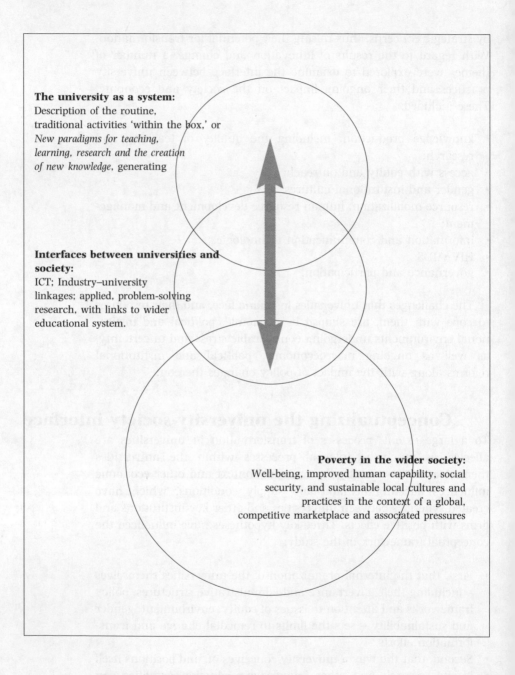

The university as a system:
Description of the routine,
traditional activities 'within the box,' or
*New paradigms for teaching,
learning, research and the creation
of new knowledge*, generating

**Interfaces between universities and
society:**
ICT; Industry–university
linkages; applied, problem-solving
research, with links to wider
educational system.

Poverty in the wider society:
Well-being, improved human capability, social
security, and sustainable local cultures and
practices in the context of a global,
competitive marketplace and associated pressures

Figure 1 Conceptual framework

increase its chances of generating dynamic synergies with the educational system, the national economy and the global market-place.

- Third – given the analysis of the country context and the continuing socio-economic and public policy trends that call for austerity – it can be seen that poverty limits funding and other resources for universities. At the same time, public austerity presents opportunities for these universities to initiate improve-ments in policies, strategies and practices targeted at producing new knowledge as well as advancing the kinds of human resources, social and scientific solutions and systems that promote improved well-being and productivity.

These hypotheses were derived in part from the presentations made by universities about their origins, mandates and vision and by their accounts of the pressures for transformation forced on them by external circumstances in the national and global marketplace. In the context of these hypotheses, the present study gives an account of the university system in Ghana by examining the extent to which routine and traditional university functions are being exercised, either:

- as coping mechanisms designed to deal with limited and shrinking human and financial resources; or
- as imaginative responses to the demands of a dynamic economy and society within a competitive global marketplace.

Throughout this study, the opportunities for new approaches to teaching, learning, research and the creation of new knowledge are examined. Examples are also introduced from other developing countries, such as India, where universities have played a key role in the ICT revolution and have generated synergies with local public and private sector economic growth. These cases suggest that certain advantages can be gained from citizens working elsewhere in the ICT field; greater industry-university linkages; applied and problem-solving research and tighter links between universities and other educational, research and policy institutions as well as local communities.

Figure 1 depicts the study's conceptual framework, and the section that follows examines the links appearing in the literature between education, poverty and development – the context in which Ghana and a majority of other African states find themselves.

Education, poverty & development

To apply the conceptual framework outlined above to Ghana, we examined the interface between education, poverty and development. Amartya Sen's *Development as Freedom* (1999) views development in its totality as expanding the real freedoms that people enjoy. This implies a broader conception of development than what is usually found in accounts that focus narrowly on the growth of the gross national product, social modernization and the like. Such accounts often evaluate whether opportunities for education and health care are 'conducive to development' in a quantitative sense. In Sen's conception, development requires the removal of major sources of what he calls *unfreedom* – poverty (defined as the lack of, or deprivation of, capability), tyranny and poor economic opportunities, as well as systematic social deprivation, intolerance and repressive regimes, in order to facilitate free agency and choice, gender equality and the development of local cultures and values. According to Sen, freedom is both a constitutive and contributory factor to stronger development outcomes (ibid.: 4, 36-40). Alongside basic freedoms of participation and expression, as well as in economic facilities and institutions, Sen highlights the crucial role of social opportunities for education and health care in expanding citizens' well-being. Using examples from Japan during the Meiji era and from other East Asian countries, Sen's analysis highlights the enhancement of economic growth through an expansion of social opportunities in education and health care, together with land reforms, in some cases even before these countries emerged from deep poverty (ibid.: 41). He demonstrates the tendency of these advances to intensify public demand from all levels of society for more innovation in the teaching, learning and research communities that universities represent.

Sen makes an important distinction between *human capital* (Schultz, 1961; Becker 1964, cited in Assie-Lumumba, 2001) and *human capability* (Sen, 1999: 293–5). In the former, there is a concentration on increasing human productive capacities, while the latter focuses on the freedom of people to lead valuable and satisfying lives and to improve their choices. Although the two concepts are related, they are not identical: the concept of human capability is broader and more inclusive, and invites a more integrated approach. In relation to education, the social benefits of education exceed its impact on human capital with respect to increasing commodity production. In our opinion, it is when education transcends the more discrete benefits of commodity production through human capital to one of increased possibilities for the enhancement of all human capabilities that transformation in the more general sense takes place. In the conceptual model depicted in Figure 1, this occurs with the development of new paradigms for teaching, learning and research. For education to have a truly catalytic role, however, investment needs to be sufficient in all levels of education as well as in funding for research, as illustrated by experiences from South-East Asia.

As is well known in the development literature, comparisons are often made between Ghana and South Korea, which were at roughly equal levels of human and social development during the early 1960s with per capita GNP of around $230, but showing very different levels of development by the late 1990s (cf. Kennedy, 1993). Thus, while Ghana's socio-economic development during the last 30 years has stagnated, that of South Korea has been remarkably strong. With a per capita GNP of over $5,000, South Korea is now firmly established as a middle-income country. However, as noted by Mkandawire and Soludo (1999), such comparisons ignore the concept of 'path dependence' as an important feature of growth, where an economy's overall performance depends critically on its point of departure, and where large qualitative differences can arise from negligible changes in initial conditions or events. Thus, in relation to Ghana and South Korea, mention should also be made of their different colonial experiences and their varied impacts, as well as the different paths to statehood and various cultural elements. In the particular case of South Korea, the aftermath of the Korean war and the country's strategic location ensured the flow of resources from Western nations in their efforts to demonstrate the superiority of its economic and political model over that of North Korea.

Mkandawire (2001) has also highlighted several policy options pursued by Asian countries, including the significant role of the state as a political and economic actor in regulated markets, that were abandoned or ruled out for African countries due to strict donor conditionality. It is therefore ironic that the same donors now constantly refer to Asian countries as shining examples for implementing the same strategies that they formerly reviled. Important differences can also be identified between the two countries' educational systems. South Korea's choice of language and writing system distinguishes its educational system from that of its Ghanaian counterpart. Korean as a language of instruction and writing allows for a different attitude towards knowledge production and dissemination, which can then be conveyed embedded in indigenous signifying systems and subsequently perceived by students as less foreign than in a setting where teaching is exclusively carried out in what may be second or third languages for students.

A broad definition of development as enhancing human capability can broaden the perspective to include indicators other than the economic-centred GNP or income per capita, which is marred by the complete or partial exclusion of the 'informal' sector. If the basic needs of health and education are seen not merely as means to achieve growth but as ends in themselves, other success stories, best practices and examples for positive change can be added to the dominant canon.

It is also possible, however, for countries with low per capita GNP to have relatively high life expectancy rates at birth, compared with countries with higher measures of GNP per capita. In this regard, Sen's comparisons of the state of Kerala (India), China and Sri Lanka (all countries with low per capita GNP) alongside Namibia, Brazil, South Africa and Gabon, are instructive (Sen, 1999: 47). In the first three countries, the expansion of relevant social services in health and education, despite their low per capita income levels, led to impressive increases in life expectancy. Although Kerala has been less successful in raising its income levels, this does not invalidate the argument that the quality of life can be improved by such efforts. Sen also emphasizes the value of education and health care in raising economic growth, and advocates a greater focus on these social programmes even in currently poor countries, without their having to wait to 'get rich' first (ibid.: 49).

Unfortunately, Ghana's experience differs from that of Kerala or Sri Lanka in this regard. While educational expenditures occupy a sizeable share of Ghana's budget (but still remain below the average for sub-Saharan Africa), a lot of the money has been spent on emoluments, with very little going towards enduring capital improvements (Addae-Mensah, 2000: 41–2) or to human capital investments in research and capacity-building. Increased spending on higher education in Africa in general, or in Ghana specifically, has not resulted in higher national standards of living for the majority of the population or in enhancements of knowledge for local use, prompting criticisms of its relevance and of 'ivory-towerism' associated with the high costs of tertiary education.

This has led to an oft-posited zero-sum relation between primary and higher education and policy choices that have emphasized primary education over tertiary education as a means to enhance equity (cf. Republic of Ghana, 2003a). These choices have been bolstered by World Bank studies on the rates of return to education (ROREs) claiming that public returns to primary education far outweigh the social benefits of higher education and that, accordingly, more resources should be allocated to the former than the latter (World Bank, 2000). However, these claims have been challenged for their reliance on ambiguous data and for employing a static mode of analysis, since rates of return to education calculated for one period may not be valid under differing economic conditions (Mkandawire and Soludo, 1999). Even more fundamentally, ROREs have been described as a 'blunt instrument for decisions about outcomes that are dependent on rate of growth, the structural transformation of the economy and technological change' (ibid., 1999: 69). Certainly in the much-touted 'knowledge-economy', primary education alone will not be sufficient to bring Ghana or any other developing country into the 'knowledge society'. Another important issue concerns the overall budgets for education in several African countries, since they fail to meet the recommended UNESCO proportion of 26 per cent of total public expenditure at the national level. Were the overall budget for education higher, there would be less pressure to choose between basic and university education, particularly in the case of females whose educational skills need improvement in order to expand the potential pool for enrolment into more advanced educational programmes (Pereira, 2002).

The perceived irrelevance of university education and of its attendant products has often been criticized. Since independence, massive investments at all levels of the educational system have been based on assumptions that they would yield many social benefits.

13

University education was seen as the channel for society and its members to emerge from poverty through its application to solving problems in production, living conditions, technology and general skills. In Ghana's recent experience, university education has provided a means for social and professional mobility for those who benefit from it, including the highly valued opportunity to leave the country for better-paid employment, resulting in a massive brain drain from the Ghanaian economy. Studies quoted in Black et al. (2003) suggest that 15 per cent of Ghanaians with tertiary education have migrated to the United States and another 10 per cent to other OECD countries, while less than 1 per cent of Ghanaians with secondary or primary education were found to have moved to OECD countries. It could also be argued, however, that Ghana and other nations reap benefits from higher education through the emigration of nationals, such as remittances, which were estimated in 2002 at $1.4 billion, well above total official development assistance (ODA) and foreign direct investment (FDI) (*Daily Graphic*, 20 August 2003).

A growing contest over the issue of 'relevance' separates those who want more relevance in university education to individuals' personal and professional benefits from those seeking relevance in relation to wider societal needs. An increasing tension over the local relevance of universities and their products has been evident in recent debates. A comment by a University of Ghana student that 'medical students are writing their exams with their tickets in their pockets' (*Ghana TV News*, 19 October 2001) reflects the reality that many of Ghana's medical graduates are bound for destinations outside the country. More than eight months later, another group of students commented that 'the conditions under which students study in Ghanaian medical schools are so appalling that this does not serve as an incentive to stay after completion' ('Ghana Medical Students Union press conference', *Daily Graphic*, 13 June 2002).

Overall, higher education in Africa generally, and in Ghana in particular, has experienced significant changes, but has not been perceived as transformational. The result has been that Ghana's efforts to fashion a development agenda in accordance with World Bank and other donors' strategies for poverty reduction have led to further reductions in expenditures on higher education. The challenge thus posed is to investigate the responses of public universities to their increasing alienation from the process of public policy-making.

Universities & the challenge of knowledge production

Universities are basically sites and systems for knowledge production. An important way in which they affect society is through the quality of their teaching and research and the effectiveness of their contributions to policy, production and management, as well as to solving social problems (Sall et al., 2003). However, in many African countries, universities are not seen as organically linked to indigenous knowledge systems, to local communities or to industry, but are seen instead as imported institutions. Hountondji (2003) has written about the extroversion of African higher education systems – with scholarly articles, conference papers and books produced primarily for the outside world first and only secondarily for their own people – as well as about the universities' isolation from local knowledge systems. The identification of local knowledge systems as 'ethno-science' by many academics becomes an alienating process; an alternative viewpoint would be to look for ways to validate these systems in their assertions or views, in what Hountondji calls a 'reciprocal process of updating' (ibid.).

While it is widely acknowledged that African universities played their appointed role of producing needed human resources during the period of 'Africanization' and nation-building that followed decolonization – functioning more as teaching than research institutions – there is much more disagreement about their current roles and missions (Zeleza, 2003; but see also Sall et al., 2003). Furthermore, their monopoly as sites for knowledge production is also being increasingly challenged by other new centres of knowledge production established within civil society, often designed expressly to meet the needs of donors and policy-makers. A more critical view has questioned the universities' monopoly status, when it is known that several indigenous systems of knowledge production exist in local communities, with few or no links to universities (Pereira, 2002). The poor quality of life for most Africans, low agricultural and industrial productivity, growing poverty and unemployment and technological backwardness are perceived to be an indictment of the

15

will and ability of universities to invest directly in Africa's social and economic development. But as Sall et al. (2003:128) observe, the public university 'is potentially one of those institutions of civil society that may help in holding the state and business sector accountable while potentially providing a source of debate on current directions and visions of society's future'.

Zeleza has pointed out that in the immediate post-independence era:

Nation-building and developmentalism became the central paradigms in African and Africanist research ... each social science discipline, from anthropology and history to economics and political science, sought to chronicle the teleological march of African cultures, societies, economies and polities from 'tradition' to 'modernity', and many believed in the importance of basic research in promoting scientific and technological development (2003: 74).

He notes, however, that, in addition to politics, structural forces also emerged with the slowdown of economic growth in the 1970s and in response to the largely successful nation-building agenda of the universities. Given the small size of the economies of many African countries, this was seen as a 'loss of mission' by state bureaucrats. Furthermore, with economic decline and the introduction of Structural Adjustment Programmes (SAPs) in the 1980s coincident with the drying up of basic research funds for universities, consultancies took the place of research at many of these institutions. As many scholars have noted (Zeleza, 2003; Mamdani, 2002; Ajayi et al., 1996), SAPs undermined both the autonomy of academics and the capability of many universities to support basic research. Universities came under attack for not 'adapting to new contexts or for being isolated' (Sall et al., 2003: 130) by governments which too often undertook repressive measures against them. The ensuing emigration of lecturers and other academic staff from these socio-economic conditions placed high burdens on those left behind to teach increasing numbers of students. Luhanga (1993, cited in Ajayi et al., 1996) catalogues the following effects of this brain drain:

- staff losses leading to additional workloads for those remaining;
- increased need for costly staff development programmes;
- negative impact on the quality of university teaching and research, leading to erosion of university enterprise;

16

- impaired training of essential medical and engineering staff, resulting in lower quality of those trained;
- expensive infrastructure remaining idle and needed research undone, thwarting institutions from making needed advances in science, technology and other developmental fields;
- deteriorating effects on university administration, especially in innovation and creativeness, due to ensuing loss of senior staff and leading to greater dependence on external sources;
- many universities left with junior, inexperienced and insufficiently trained staff, further impairing their capacity for knowledge production and dissemination.

In addition, the deplorable state of libraries and laboratories in many universities has damaged their natural sciences programmes, while in the social sciences it may have encouraged some students to do more research in their own communities. As Mamdani has noted, at Makerere University in the 1980s and 1990s students were encouraged to collect and analyze data from their home areas (Mamdani, 2002). Mostly, however, applied research in the service of nation-building was favoured over basic research, and there was also an increased reliance on foreign experts in development research.

According to Zeleza (2003) an ironic situation was created where many governments had access to the expertise of their own academics only through donor-contracted reports! There were also rate-of-return studies questioning the effectiveness of universities combined with an increased reliance on major research foundations for support and research, with the attendant risk of losing control over the research agenda. Under such conditions, Mamdani's report on research activities and knowledge production in African universities compared with the situation in OECD countries is revealing: he notes that OECD countries enjoy extensive government research funding, with about 80 per cent of research funded in this way. Using UNESCO figures, he shows that, of 900 African titles produced in 2001, only 1.5 per cent were published in Africa, and, of these, 65 per cent were published in South Africa and 25 per cent in North Africa, reflecting both a dearth of research and its ensuing relevance for advancing the learning process in Africa (Mamdani, 2002). Knowledge production takes place through research and teaching activities, which in turn allows students and others to make better

17

choices and demands on their teachers and to build new capabilities.

An important issue raised by Sall et al. (2003) concerns the challenges of globalization for knowledge production, which is particularly valid for Ghana. They note that a major reason for increased attention to higher education is the belief in knowledge as the 'glue' and 'fuel' of the new global economy and that, once again, Africans will miss out if they do not pay more attention to the production of knowledge. An equal concern of African governments is that, despite their investments in higher education, their citizens may not reap benefits from these investments, since highly skilled nationals will probably emigrate, further impairing each nation's ability to advance its own economy. Nonetheless, Sall et al. underscore the importance of focusing on the 'knowledge economy' due to the incontrovertible fact:

... that knowledge matters for a range of socio-political issues that play out in the public sphere – an informed citizenry, independent media, a space for public intellectual debate, the forging of social networks that facilitate cooperation and collective action, the forging of a 'human rights culture'.... We need not accept the more utopian versions of the knowledge society to take seriously the role that knowledge may play in the constitution of the public sphere (ibid.: 135).

An important dimension of this public sphere has been identified in this study's conceptual framework as the point at which the university interfaces with society and the broader educational system in a synergistic manner, such that new paradigms of learning, teaching and research may emerge.

An area of importance that has been neglected until very recently is the place of gender in the African intellectual landscape. African feminist scholars have critiqued the male domination of African universities and the creation of academic environments unfriendly to women either as students or staff members (Mama, 2002; Pereira, 2002; Bennett, 2002; Kwesiga, 2002). The misogyny on many campuses, the low proportion of female students and the even lower percentage of female academics and administrators across the continent highlight the unequal inclusion of women in education and reinforce the image of many African universities as old boys' networks. Not surprisingly, with few exceptions, female perspectives have not permeated the 'malestream' of scholarship. Mama notes that:

18

In Africa, as much as anywhere else, the public university remains the key site for the production of knowledge and expertise. It is also the key site for the production and reproduction of values and world-views, for the production of people, of identities, subjectivities and consciousness. Yet this clearly ideological role has most often been covert, in keeping with the liberal political tradition, and its claims to neutrality (2003:10).

The needed transformations in African universities and societies cannot occur without confronting these modern 'traditions' and value systems that denigrate and exploit women and keep them out of scholarship and academia. The efforts of a growing network of Africa-based feminist scholars to turn a gendered lens on their institutional environments and to integrate issues of identity, sexuality and culture represent first steps to generate locally grounded theory and practice and infuse them into the curriculum (AGI, 2002). These issues are taken up further in Chapter 9.

The growing menace of the HIV/AIDS pandemic, and its deadly toll on African societies and universities in particular, also present an opportunity to confront the enduring silence about sexuality and power in both the curricula and the operational policies of universities, as well as to provide better leadership to society at large. Despite the heavy prevalence of transactional sex among students and staff alike on African campuses, institutions have not generally confronted the gender-related issues of sexuality and power. The reality of disease and death and their high human, emotional and institutional costs demand courageous, honest and innovative strategies and new ways of imagining and conducting gender relations, particularly on university campuses.

This study contends that the extent to which African institutions take on these issues will determine the transformations that occur and how they will spill over into the rest of the society and the economy and improve well-being, human capabilities and sustainable local cultures and practices.

2 Ghana: National Context, Socio-Economic & Political Development

Geopolitical & socio-economic background

Located in West Africa and sharing boundaries with Côte d'Ivoire, Burkina Faso and Togo, Ghana achieved independence in March 1957 and became a republic in 1960. In the years since independence, the country has weathered four military coups; December 2000 marked the first time in its history that a change of government was effected through the ballot box. Ghana operates a presidential system of government and has a 230-member Parliament, of whom only 25 are women. While its democratic process has been hailed both nationally and internationally, its economic situation is still a matter of concern.

Administratively, Ghana is divided into ten regions and 138 districts.[4] In line with the government's decentralization policy, district assemblies were established in 1988 in an effort to transfer power and competencies from the central to the local level. District assemblies are charged with implementing national policies at the local level, contextualized to suit local priorities and needs. They also have functional responsibilities for planning, resource mobilization and allocation, monitoring and evaluation, and are meant to facilitate the participation of ordinary people in governance. To enhance wider participation, arrangements have been provided for both elected and appointed members, in order to accommodate special interest groups as well as to co-opt specialized technical expertise for the benefit of assemblies. Nearly a third (30 per cent) of appointed members, who constitute one-third of assembly members, are supposed to be women.

The Ghanaian economy, SAPs and liberalization

Ghana is largely an agricultural country; 38 per cent of its gross domestic product (GDP) is derived from agriculture, and 63 per cent of the population is rural. The Ghanaian economy has been in dire straits for nearly three decades and is highly donor-dependent. From its early promise as a model economy dependent on the export of

---

[4] Some 328 new districts were recently created in line with provisions in the Local Government Act (Act 462) of 1993.

agricultural and extractive raw materials of cocoa, timber and gold (Szerezewski, 1965) and an import-substitution industrialization under the first post-independence government of Kwame Nkrumah (Killick, 1978), the economy went into a downward spiral from the early 1970s to the early 1980s, with per capita GDP declining by a total of 19.7 per cent and dropping by a further 21.2 per cent from 1980 to 1983 (Hutchful, 2002: 6). There were also sharp declines in domestic and export production, and the manufacturing index also declined remarkably, with average capacity utilization estimated at only 24 per cent by 1981. During these years, the economy additionally registered severe fiscal imbalances that were covered by excessive borrowing from both internal and external sources. Explanations for the crises place external ahead of internal causes (ibid.: 8-9); these include drought in a rainfall-dependent agricultural economy, increased fuel import costs, inflationary pressures, unfavourable terms of trade, policy distortions, poor administration and corruption. More fundamentally, as Hutchful explains, the Ghanaian economy, like many other African economies, has not altered significantly from the colonial-type 'trade economy' inherited at independence, with the following features: a strong divergence between production and consumption structures; excessive openness and vulnerability to foreign markets, with a high commodity concentration of exports; backward domestic agriculture; a prevalence of small and marginal urban and rural enterprise, and the dominance of buying and selling activities. In addition, the emergence of a parallel economy eroded the government's tax base and caused massive deterioration in social services and physical infrastructures.

The Economic Recovery Programme (ERP) initiated in 1983 by the Rawlings government, under the supervision of the World Bank and the International Monetary Fund on the structural adjustment programme model, had the main objectives of increasing production, particularly of food, industrial raw materials and exports, by improving the structure of incentives, increasing the availability of consumer goods, rehabilitating the physical infrastructure, increasing the overall availability and improving the allocation of foreign exchange, and lowering the rate of inflation through the pursuit of prudent macroeconomic policies. These measures have had mixed results at best. The focus of the first three years of the programme was mainly on stabilization, and some improvements were recorded

21

Table 1 Macroeconomic indicators, 1983–2000: annual averages

	1983	1984-86	1987-89	1990-92	1993-95	1996-98	1999	2000
GDP growth rate (%)	-4.3	6.3	5.2	4.1	4.3	4.5	4.4	3.7
Gross Fixed Investment Rate (%)	3.7	8.7	14.4	15.2	22.5	22.01	n.a.	n.a.
Average annual inflation rate (%)	123	25	32	22	36	37[a]	n.a.	n.a.
Exports (f.o.b.) US$m	439	649	838	960	1244	1717	2006	1937
Share of traditional exports (%)[b]	89	89	86	82	86	80	72	68

Notes: a) Annual average for 1996–1997; b) Cocoa and cocoa products, minerals and timber.
Sources: Ghana Statistical Services, *Quarterly Digest of Statistics*, various issues, Accra; International Monetary Fund, *International Finance Statistics Yearbook* (1994), Washington DC; Bank of Ghana, *Statistical Bulletin*, various issues, Accra; Extracted from World Bank (2003).

initially in most important macroeconomic indicators (Table 1).

Beginning in 1987, the second phase of the Economic Recovery Programme focused on structural and institutional issues. A number of reforms were launched in education, the financial sector, state enterprises and the civil service, with their attendant currency devaluations, import liberalization, retrenchment of employees, privatization of state enterprises and shrinkage in the role of the state, and in the provision of social services, including education and health. Cost-recovery measures were instituted in health and education, while under the Education Sector Reform programme, official permission was given for private providers in the tertiary sector, in accordance with the appropriate regulatory framework. According to the Ghana Poverty Reduction Strategy (Republic of Ghana, 2003a), programmes under the Structural Adjustment Programme met with some short-lived success in macroeconomic recovery and stabilization, but largely failed in structural reform. They achieved only a limited success in the growth of agriculture

22

and manufacturing and propelled an expansion in services on the back of a debt-financed import and consumption boom. The expected transformation of the export base also failed to materialize.

By the end of the 1990s, the economic situation could be summed up as follows: while in the 1970s agriculture accounted for more than half of the nation's total value added, it had declined to just over 40 per cent by the 1990s, and farm-gate expenditure on agriculture had been desultory. Industrial output also declined from about 20 to 14 per cent of Gross Domestic Product (GDP) during the same period. Services, on the other hand, rose from about 30 to 44 per cent of GDP, overtaking agriculture as the dominant sector. The sharp expansion of services coincided with a virtual disappearance of private savings during the 1980s and 1990s, while the imports/GDP ratio rose thirteen-fold, far surpassing the export/GDP ratio and opening up a wide trade gap. The public saving ratio that had improved during the 1980s under the reform programmes lapsed again into dis-saving during the 1990s. The reform programmes also left in their wake large and persistent fiscal and trade deficits, with the former creating a heavy debt burden while the external gaps put severe pressure on the balance of payments. In the 1990s growth was stable, but never exceeded 5 per cent a year. Gross investment rates were also fairly constant, remaining in the range of 20-23 per cent, and exports continued to grow more rapidly than GDP, despite the decreasing weight of traditional exports.

In spite of the growth of the economy and exports, the economy has remained dependent on external financial assistance, and concerns have been expressed about the limited impact of the reforms on employment creation. Overall, donors contributed the largest share of non-wage expenditure. This portion represented 75 per cent of total non-wage expenditure in 1997 but declined to about 66 per cent in 1998. According to the GPRS (Republic of Ghana, 2003a), donor aid to economic services and infrastructure represented a substantial proportion of total expenditure in these two areas for 2001, as follows: agriculture, 86 per cent; water, 76 per cent; energy, 90 per cent; roads, 76 per cent; industry, 72 per cent. This level of donor support is considered unsustainable in the long term and points to the limited impact of the reform programmes in diversifying the structure of the economy. Thus the years 1999 and 2000, which witnessed the combination of a decline in cocoa and gold prices, rising oil prices and a shortfall in expected external inflows, affected the economy adversely and resulted in a fiscal crisis. By the end of 1999, the build-up of arrears was estimated to be about 5 per cent of GDP (CEPA, 2000). With elections at the end of 2000 and the coming to power of a new administration led by President John Kuffour, the government declared that it had no other recourse but to seek relief under the HIPC Initiative.

Poverty and the Heavily Indebted Poor Countries Initiative

Ghana opted to join the HIPC Initiative in March 2001 with a per capita income of US$390 and an external debt totalling $6.2 billion. The country's poor economic performance over the last two decades, despite its consistent adherence to a structural adjustment pro-gramme, is reflected in the living standards of its citizens. Today 40 per cent of the population of 20 million is defined as poor and 27 per cent as living in extreme poverty, although there are important regional and locational differences. Five out of the ten regions in Ghana had more than 40 per cent of their population living in

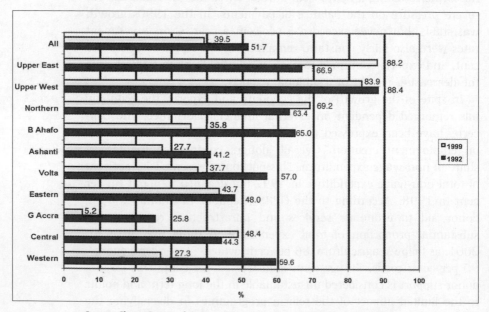

Source: Ghana Statistical Service, *Poverty Trends in the 1990s*, Accra, 2000.

Figure 2 Regional poverty profiles in Ghana

poverty in 1999, with the worst affected being the three northern savannah regions (the Upper East, Upper West and Northern Regions). Nine out of ten people in the Upper East Region, eight out of ten in the Upper West and seven out of ten in the Northern Region were classified as poor in 1999, in comparison with five out of ten in the Central and Eastern Regions (see Figure 2).

Of the ten regions, the Upper East, Northern and Central regions experienced increases in poverty and extreme poverty in the 1990s, while urban areas in the northern savannah also experienced signifi- cant increases in poverty during the period.

The adult literacy rate is currently 54 per cent, with a dispro- portionate rate of 46 per cent for females and 63 per cent for males. The United Nations' *Human Development Index* (HDI) ranked Ghana 129 out of 179 countries for 2003, while the UNDP gender-related development index (GDI) ranked it 104 out of 144 countries, demon- strating the wide gender disparities in Ghana's social and economic life. Some 35 per cent of Ghanaians have no access to safe water and only 45 per cent have access to basic sanitation; 40 per cent of the total population live more than 15 km from a health facility, and many health facilities do not have a full range of services due to staff shortages and maldistribution of skilled personnel. While these

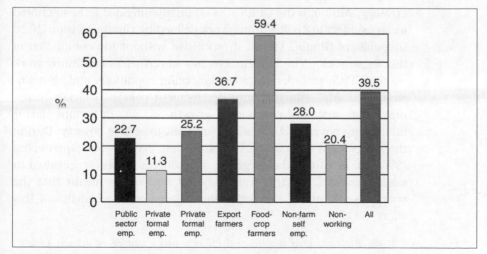

Source: ibid.

Figure 3: Poverty by socio-economic groups

figures have not been further disaggregated by gender, it is clear that the rural and urban poor are disproportionately affected, among whom are several million women.

As Figure 3 illustrates, poverty is highest among food-crop farmers, and the contribution of this group to the national incidence of poverty is reported to be far in excess of their population size (Republic of Ghana, 2003a). The incidence of poverty is also high among export farmers, informal sector employees and the non-farm self-employed.

Government expenditure has been biased in favour of recurrent expenditure, approximately 30 per cent of which goes on salaries. The level of expenditure in the social sector is low relative to African averages, with spending on health and education at 2.0 and 2.8 per cent of GDP, respectively. Education and health account for about 90 per cent of social sector spending, while the remaining sub-sectors each receive a small proportion of funds.

Ghana's medium-term development & poverty reduction strategy

Both the dimensions of poverty and the prevailing economic paradigms under which it has grown have found expression in the critiques that have been aimed at the Ghana Poverty Reduction Strategy. Although the GPRS was originally intended to be anchored in an overarching policy framework defined by Ghana's Vision 2020 (Republic of Ghana, 1995), it proceeded without the completion of this framework.[5] The government has nevertheless continued work on the GPRS, in order to reflect emerging conditions and to main-stream poverty reduction into development policies. Officials recognize that sustained economic growth is an important factor influencing poverty, but it is not sufficient to reduce poverty. During the adjustment period, the emphasis on Sector-wide Approaches (SWAps), involving the targeting of resources by sector, resulted in modest growth, but this trend has not necessarily meant that the poorest segments of the population shared in the benefits of this effort.

[5] Vision 2020 has been shelved, and the new policy framework defining Ghana's Medium-term Development Goals is not yet in place. The constitutional requirement is that the new government is expected to present this to Parliament no more than two years after coming into office.

The GPRS has five main components:

- macroeconomic stability;
- production and gainful employment;
- human resources development (including education) and basic services;
- vulnerability and exclusion;
- governance.

The GPRS is founded on the government's medium-term priorities of infrastructural development, a modernized agriculture based on rural development, enhanced social services, good governance and private sector development. These are to be achieved by ensuring sound economic management for accelerated growth, increasing production and promoting sustainable livelihoods, directly supporting human development and the provision of basic services, providing special programmes in support of the vulnerable and excluded, guaranteeing good governance and increased service capacity in the public sector and through the active involvement of the private sector as the main engine of growth and a partner in nation-building. The GPRS particularly emphasizes the need to trigger economic growth through accelerated and job-creating agro-based industrial growth.

The GPRS has been criticized on several fronts. A major critique has been that it is firmly anchored in the neo-liberal framework that has failed to deliver after more than 20 years of structural adjustment programming, and that it is more a condition for accessing the HIPC Initiative than a 'country-owned' strategy. There is also concern over the lack of a pro-poor or pro-gender focus in the GPRS approach, which prioritizes wealth creation and growth in ways that favour middle-income groups rather than the poor, making the former the main beneficiaries of interventions. Growth targets and projections in several sectors under the GPRS are seen as over-optimistic and not based on reliable data; this is particularly true of the growth projections in the agricultural sector, whose growth is expected to finance a large proportion of the GPRS interventions. This has led to growing apprehensions about the possibility of realistically achieving the needed economic growth and about its impacts on the poorest groups in Ghana. Another major concern over the GPRS is its relation to the national budget and its public

27

allocations and its capacity to serve the poor. Like the national budget, the GPRS is also heavily reliant on donor funding, raising further questions about sustainability.

Education in the GPRS

Critical in the evolution of the GPRS and the medium-term development agenda are the roles of education in general, and higher education in particular, with respect to policy initiatives and the influence that universities have had on them.

Education strategy under the GPRS addresses the lack of progress during the 1990s in increasing enrolment and raising quality in basic education. It focuses on the following fundamental issues: wide inequalities in access to and quality of basic education; shortfalls in spending; extremely limited and restrictive non-salary expenditures and acute management gaps, particularly in teacher deployment and supervision, distribution of learning materials, retention of qualified personnel and co-ordination of donor support.

The strategy places a renewed emphasis on developing basic education, since half of the Ghanaian population is unable to write a simple letter. Access to basic education is to be supported by early childhood development and alternative educational options for children out of school, with emphasis on the hard-to-reach areas of northern Ghana, remote rural areas and the urban slums.

Table 2 sets out the indicative targets for the education sector under the GPRS.

While spending on basic education should, of course, be increased to ensure its provision to all children, it is unfortunate that the old zero-sum game between basic and higher education persists at the same time as the government is eager to reduce poverty and achieve higher human resource development. Basic education is increasingly pitched against supposedly ineffective and unnecessary higher education. Given the Ghanaian government's donor dependence and the negative attitude of donors towards higher education, which is not seen as complementing, enhancing and supporting basic education, this view may prove more decisive. Neither of these goals, however, can be achieved without rapid development and increased spending in ICT and in higher education. The proposed spending cuts in teacher education are also unfortunate, given the large numbers of untrained teachers – more than 50 per cent of teachers

Table 2: Education targets in the GPRS, 2002–04 (%)

Target	2001	2004	Percentage Change
% of total government spending on education	16.9	19.5	2.6
% of total education spending on:			
Primary (KG and primary)	33	36	3
Junior secondary	19	20	1
Secondary	11	11	–
Vocational	1.6	2	0.4
Teacher training	6	5	(-1)
Other tertiary education	15	12	(-3)
Gross primary school enrolment rate			
total	77.6	82	4.4
girls	71	80	9
Gross junior secondary school enrolment rate	61	65	4
Gross senior secondary school enrolment rate	17	25	8
Primary school drop-out rate at primary:			
girls	30	20	–10
boys	20	10	-10
Primary 6 pass rates for Criterion Referenced Tests at mastery level for public schools:			
English	8.3		
Maths	4.7		
Transition rate from P6 to Junior Secondary School	96	98	2
Transition rate from JSS to SSS/ technical	35	40	5
Children reached by alternative education in Accra, Kumasi, three northern regions		100,000	

Source: Republic of Ghana, 2003a.

in basic and secondary education, according to the Report of the President's Committee on the Review of Education Reforms in Ghana (Republic of Ghana, 2002a). The expansion of vocational and technical education will also require more graduates from the polytechnics, which are part of the tertiary education sector. University graduates are needed to teach in the polytechnics as well as to support the emerging private universities, many of which do not engage in any staff training. The bias against tertiary education also makes it impossible to match the funds earmarked for education with sufficient growth in university enrolments and the broader needs for university development and expansion, as will be discussed in Chapter 6 below. What is clearly needed, then, is a comprehensive framework for education that examines the system as a whole and aligns it with broader development needs, as presented in the conceptual framework outlined in Chapter 1.

The challenge of poverty in Ghana is real, and radical measures are needed for its eradication. The role that education plays in that effort has also been documented in the experience of many other countries. Unfortunately, in Ghana the exigencies of funding the education sector, itself a function of growing poverty, have narrowed the debate on the roles and functions of education for national and self-development. As a low-income country, Ghana cannot afford to have its basic schools churn out annually tens of thousands of poorly educated and low-skilled youth, many of whom end up as urban slum dwellers, chasing non-existent jobs and perpetuating the cycle of poverty and growing inequality. In this regard, synergies need to be developed between tertiary education and other levels in the education sector, as well as between education and industry, communities, other knowledge-production centres and government. In the remaining chapters of this study, we examine how the public universities are rising to these challenges and what more might be done to accelerate such efforts.

3 The System of Higher Education

Education in Ghana, both formal and informal, is both highly treasured and rewarded, and it has played crucial roles in social advancement and in the society at large (see Addae-Mensah, 2000). As Yankah (1995) has observed, pre-colonial Ghanaian societies valued those who were well versed in the traditions of a community and could apply them to solving contemporary local problems; these people were often elevated to honoured positions, even when they were of lowly origin.

The demand for formal education in Ghana, as in most African countries, has been high. This has come from students, parents and social groups that have traditionally lacked access to the educational system and from governments anxious to satisfy the claims of increasingly vocal groups (see Sall et al., 2003). These calls have led to pressures for the expansion of educational resources. Nevertheless, enrolment ratios in universities for young people aged between 20 and 24 in Africa are still the lowest in the world. According to UNESCO projections, only 2.6 per cent of Ghanaian pupils who enter primary school eventually make it to the tertiary level (Republic of Ghana, 1999, cited in Addae-Mensah, 2000:38).

In some countries, such as Nigeria and Ghana, new public universities have also been created in response to regional demands for access, leading to an impressive rise in enrolments. However, many of these institutions have been poorly capitalized and offer only the pretence of a university education. More importantly, the increased enrolments hide structural inequalities based on age, region, social class, gender, ethnicity and rural/urban origin that determine access to university education. These structural inequalities reflect historical patterns established under colonial rule when formal education systems were introduced, and have been continued in varying degrees by post-independence systems of education that made no structural reforms to the content and orientation of schooling. Thus regions and social groups with better access to primary and secondary education have typically registered higher enrolments at tertiary levels (cf. Addae-Mensah, 2000). The combined effects of ethnicity, religion and region have also been reflected in educational achievement and representation, with southern, Christianized urban regions often enjoying better access to these resources than northern, Muslim rural regions. Writing specifically on the differential access to education, Assie-Lumumba (2001) has commented that policies and actions in the educational sector have also favoured younger students, and that age has acted as a proxy for social class, with social class and student ages being negatively correlated.

The institutions

The tertiary education sector in Ghana is currently made up of universities – both public and private – colleges, polytechnics, institutes and schools. The full list of institutions accredited by the National Accreditation Board (NAB) as at January 2004 includes the following:

Universities: University of Ghana, Kwame Nkrumah University of Science and Technology, University of Cape Coast, University for Development Studies and University of Education, Winneba (all public).[6]

University Colleges: Western University College (public), and Central University College, Methodist University College, All Nations University College, Catholic University College of Ghana, Islamic University College, Presbyterian University College, Wisconsin International University College, Valley View University College and Ashesi University College (all private).

Polytechnics: Accra Polytechnic, Cape Coast Polytechnic, Ho Polytechnic, Takoradi Polytechnic, Tamale Polytechnic, Kumasi Polytechnic, Koforidua Polytechnic, Sunyani Polytechnic, Wa Polytechnic and Bolgatanga Polytechnic (all public).

Professional institutions: Ghana Institute of Management and

[6] The University of Ghana has established Workers' Colleges in all ten regions of the country. The UEW has also developed Distance Education Centres that provide opportunities for students to access university courses without being enrolled at the main campuses. In 2005, UEW changed its name from University College of Education.

Table 3: Enrolment in public tertiary institutions for 2003 and 2004

Institutions	2003	2004	Change in enrolment	% change in enrolment
Universities				
Univ. of Ghana	17893	23898	6005	33.56
KNUST	11976	13391	1415	11.82
Univ. of Cape Coast	11637	12735	1096	9.44
Univ. of Educ. Winneba	9909	9915	6	0.06
Univ. of Devt Studies	1796	2765	969	53.95
Western Univ. Coll	684	872	188	27.49
Total	53895	63576	9681	17.96
Polytechnics				
Accra	4005	4845	840	20.97
Kumasi	2930	2985	55	1.88
Takoradi	3131	3236	105	3.35
Ho	1822	1837	15	0.82
Cape Coast	3222	3203	-19	-0.59
Tamale	4490	4429	-61	-1.36
Sunyani	1946	1889	-57	- 2.93
Koforidua	1571	1728	157	9.99
Wa	0	51	51	0.00
Bolgatanga	0	150	150	0.00
Total	23117	24353	1236	5.35
Professional Institutes				
IPS	538	551	13	2.42
GIL	71	119	48	67.61
Total	609	670	61	10.02
Grand total	77621	88599	10978	14.14

Source: NCTE, 2004.

Public Administration (GIMPA); the Institute of Professional Studies (IPS); National Film and Television Institute (NAFTI); Ghana Institute of Journalism (GIJ); teacher training colleges; selected nursing training and teacher training colleges (all public) and the Academy of Screen Arts (private).

Distance-Learning Institutions: Resource Development International (RDI), University of South Africa (UNISA), Ghana College and Kludjeson Institute of Technology (KIT) (the latter two are both local private institutions).

Tutorial Colleges: Academy of Business Administration, Ghana School of Marketing, Graduate School of Management, Institute of Management Studies, Intercom Programming and Manufacturing Company (IPMC), NIIT Education and Training Centre, Premier Institute of Law Enforcement Management and Administration, West Africa Computer Science Institute and Zenith College (all private)

Theological Colleges: Akrofi-Christaller Memorial Centre for Mission Research and Applied Theology (postgraduate studies and research), Ghana Baptist Theological Seminary, Ghana Christian College and Seminary, Christian Service College, Maranatha Bible College and Trinity Theological Seminary (all private).

In addition to the above, there are nearly 100 private tertiary institutions that have applied to the NAB for certification (Republic of Ghana, 2002a).

Table 3 shows student enrolment levels in public tertiary institutions in 2003 and 2004. It is noteworthy that there were dramatic increases in enrolment at the University of Ghana, the University for Development Studies (UDS) and the Western University College (WUC), well above the maximum 10 per cent increase per year suggested by the National Council for Tertiary Education (NCTE). However, both UDS and WUC have relatively small enrolments and may be said to be in their growth periods. The huge increase in enrolment in light of limited resources is a matter of concern that has negative implications for the adequate provision of facilities and quality assurance in the institutions. This is examined further in Chapter 4.

The establishment & growth of public universities

Ghana's system of formal higher education was begun with the establishment of the University College of the Gold Coast in 1948, as a college of the University of London, to offer programmes in the humanities, arts, sciences and agriculture. It was followed by the Kumasi College of Technology in 1952, with a mandate to under-

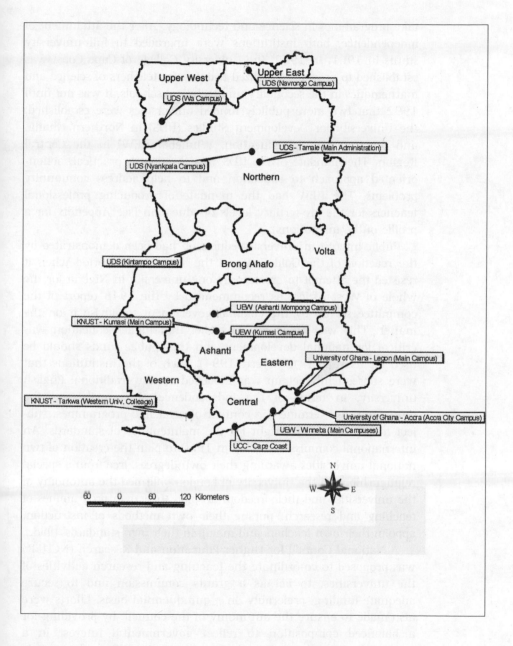

Figure 4: Location of public universities in Ghana

take programmes in science and technology. After the attainment of independence, both institutions were upgraded to full university status in 1961. In 1962, the University College of Cape Coast was established to provide specialized training for teachers of science and mathematics in the secondary and technical schools. It was not until 1992 that two more publicly funded universities were established: the University for Development Studies (UDS) in Northern Ghana, and the University of Education, Winneba (UEW) in the Central Region. The mandate of the UDS was to adopt a practical, action-oriented approach to education and to help address community problems. The UEW had the mandate of producing professional teachers for the pre-tertiary levels of education (see Appendix for a profile of the institutions).

Public interest in university education had been demonstrated by the reaction of the Gold Coast in the late colonial period when it resisted the attempt to create only one university in Nigeria for the whole of West Africa, as recommended by the 1946 report of the committee set up by the colonial government to advise it on the matter. This was based on the belief that higher education was critical for national development and that public funds should be used for its support (Sawyerr, 1994). Each of the institutions that were subsequently set up was modelled on the traditional English university, in terms of the independence of councils and the autonomy to determine the content of academic programmes, subject to appropriate oversight for the maintenance of standards. An international commission set up in 1960 to plan the creation of two national universities awarding their own degrees, free from a special relationship with the University of London, affirmed the autonomy of the universities and their freedom 'to plan their own programmes of teaching and research, pursue their own methods of instruction, appoint their own teachers and maintain their own standards' (ibid.).

A National Council for Higher Education and Research (NCHER) was proposed to co-ordinate the teaching and research activities of the universities, to act as a grants commission and to secure adequate funding, preferably on a quinquennial basis. Efforts were also made to ensure the autonomy of the council, by providing for a balanced composition to reflect governmental interest in a university responsive to its environment, its scientific and academic pursuits and those of other research institutions (Sawyerr, 1994).

While the NCHER has gone through some changes, this has not affected its essential functions (see Chapter 8). The most significant developments in the legal framework of public university governance have been Provisional National Defence Council (PNDC) Law 42 of 1982 and PNDC Law 239 of 1990. The first mandated the inclusion of students and workers on University Councils, while the second made the Head of State Chancellor of the university and the Vice-Chancellor appointable by the ruling government on the recommendation of the University Council. The advent of the Fourth Republican Constitution in 1992 removed these powers from the government and returned authority to appoint the Chancellor and Vice-Chancellor to the University Councils, even as it retained the expanded composition introduced by PNDC Law 42.

The policy environment

The policy environment within which the universities operate has been defined in a number of documents, including the 1992 Constitution of the Republic, Vision 2020 and the sector-wide strategic plan of the Ministry of Education.

The 1992 Constitution enshrines the right to education in Article 25 as follows:

- basic education is free, compulsory and available to all;
- secondary education, including technical, vocational education and training, is to be generally available and accessible and will be progressively made free;
- higher education is also 'equally accessible to all, on the basis of capacity' and will be progressively made free;
- functional literacy is to be encouraged and intensified.

The following objectives relating to education were contained in the Vision 2020 document:

- improving learning achievement;
- increasing school enrolments;
- improving retention;
- reducing geographical disparities in the provision of education;
- improving teacher quality;

- continuing curricular reform to make education more relevant;
- expanding tertiary education;
- increasing literacy rates;
- improving the efficient management of resource use.

The Ministry of Education (MOE) is responsible for translating national education goals for human development into policy. The two main agencies under the ministry responsible for implementing policy measures are the Ghana Education Service, responsible for pre-tertiary education, and the National Council for Tertiary Education, responsible for tertiary education. There are also other educational oversight organizations under the ministry, such as the West African Examinations Council, the Ghana Library Board, the Ghana Book Development Council, the National Service Scheme and the Ghana National Commission on UNESCO, which are responsible for other key functions relating to examinations, quality and the ongoing contribution of the recipients of free education to national development. The MOE's mission is stated as follows:

... to provide relevant education to all Ghanaians at all levels irrespective of gender, ethnic, religious and political affiliation. In providing the services, the Ministry is guided by the values of quality education, efficient management of resources, accountability and transparency (Republic of Ghana, Ministry of Education, 2001:4).

Within the strategic plan of the MOE, the specific objectives for the tertiary sector have been formulated as follows:

- to improve access to participation in education and extend educational opportunities;
- to improve the quality and relevance of academic programmes;
- to extend the provision of technology and science education;
- to strengthen the governance, planning and resource management of tertiary education and make these institutions more efficient and effective (ibid.: 5).

The achievement of these policy objectives is constrained by the availability of both financial and human resources. The continuing controversy over these principles as well as over the autonomy of the institutions has been reflected in government-university relations over the years.

Government-university relations during three periods

Sawyerr (1994) identifies three phases in government-university relations in Ghana: the period of the First Republic, 1957–66; the periods of military rule, 1966–81; and the period from 1981 to 1992.

The state control model: the period of the First Republic, 1957–66

The first phase was the period immediately following independence in which higher education was invested with the task of Africanizing the public services in Ghana and playing a critical role in national self-discovery, culture and sovereignty (see also Zeleza, 2003). The establishment of the Institute of African Studies at the University of Ghana under the personal direction of President Nkrumah, the Encyclopedia Africana project under the direction of W.E.B. Du Bois and the setting up of the Ghana Institute of Public Administration (GIMPA), the Ghana Medical School, the University College of Science Education (later the University of Cape Coast) and the Council for Scientific and Industrial Research with its several institutes were seen as critical in accelerating the pace of Africanization and the goals of national independence, and in meeting the growing needs of the new nation.

As Sawyerr (1994) points out, the government of newly independent Ghana took great pride in its universities and provided generously for them. But there was also impatience with what was seen as the elitism, conservatism and bureaucratic processes in the universities, particularly at the University of Ghana. Government attempts to exercise greater control than was deemed desirable by the academic community set it on a collision course with the universities. Government intervention in certain appointments and promotions, and the dismissal and deportation of some expatriate professors, was deeply resented, and many members of the University of Ghana applauded the coup that overthrew the Nkrumah government in 1966. On the other hand, the Kwame Nkrumah University of Science and Technology and the University of Cape Coast, with their focus on science and technology, which was more in line with the government's emphasis on accelerated development based on greater application of science and

39

technology, were perceived as less political and did not experience serious conflict with the government authorities. In the classic strategy to 'reward your friends and punish your enemies', the Institute of Education at the University of Ghana was removed to the University of Cape Coast on the orders of the President, while the government appointed a chief and former minister of culture as the Vice-Chancellor of the University of Ghana, attesting to Sawyerr's characterization of this phase as a 'state control model' (ibid.: 7).

The state-supervised model, 1966–81

The second phase in government-university relations covers the period from 1966 to 1981 and was largely a period of military rule, with brief interludes of civilian rule from 1969 to 1972 and again from 1979 to 1981. During this time, there were no major attempts to 'control' the universities, but it was a period during which the fortunes of these institutions diminished significantly, and they experienced varying periods of disruption in their academic schedules as a result of deteriorating economic, political and social conditions. These difficulties led to stringent budget cuts for the universities, and the public services in general, and greater involvement of various sections of the university community, principally students, in the restoration of democracy in Ghana. The rapidly deteriorating economic situation also led to an exodus of lecturers and other university personnel, accompanied by a serious loss of confidence and morale in the universities. Sawyerr (1994) attributes the continuing decline in the effectiveness of universities as institutions of higher learning in Ghana to this period.

Despite these tribulations, Sawyerr asserts that the procedural and substantive autonomy of the universities remained essentially intact during this second phase. Thus, while these institutions had undergone substantial changes in their modes of operation, had expanded in size and enrolment and had added new faculties and departments, Sawyerr maintains that they still retained the basic ideology and characteristic features of the traditional English university, with the autonomous power to determine their academic procedures and internal administration. While the government still determined their budgetary grants, the universities retained the power to allocate them to different programmes within the university. Sawyerr des-

40

cribes this model as one of state supervision, in place of the state control under the Nkrumah regime. He notes three factors that have been critical in government-university relations. First there was the fragmented organizational style, the traditions of academic freedom and the dispersal of decision-making power among the principal officers, senior professoriate and committee systems in the universities that allowed these institutions to resist outside pressure, unless such pressure either became overwhelming or matched already-existing alignments within the institution. The second factor that strongly influenced government-university relations was the leadership calibre of the university, including its stature, diplomatic skills and willingness to stand up to government pressure. The third reinforcing factor has been the popular esteem that universities in Ghana have always enjoyed, which regimes in power have also understood (see Sall et al., 2003).

Confrontation and directed change: The Provisional National Defence Council (PNDC) era, 1981–92

The third phase in university-government relations occurred under the military regime of Flight-Lieutenant Jerry Rawlings, which was marked by very difficult economic, social and political conditions, culminating in the ERP/SAP discussed in Chapter 2. Initially students, workers and some lecturers supported the regime, while the universities were closed for almost a year to allow students to help with the evacuation of cocoa from the countryside to the ports. Furthermore, the composition of university councils was amended by decree during this period to allow student and worker participation. However, soon thereafter relations between the regime and the universities went through severe trials, as Sawyerr (1994) recounts. The National Council on Higher Education was abolished in 1983 and replaced by the Higher Education Division of the Ministry of Education and Culture, which was set up to co-ordinate higher education under the advice of a newly established Education Commission. It was also during this period that the Committee of Vice-Chancellors (CVC) began to play an increasingly important role in government-university relations, particularly in relation to the conditions of service for staff and in the government's relations with students. This committee also allowed the heads of public universities to develop a unified position when dealing with the government.

41

Table 4: Staff members at the University of Ghana

	1980/81	1981/2	1983/4	1985/6	1987/8
Academic	523	504	422	488	578
Non-academic		3,488	3,062	3,141	3,178
Total		3,992	3,484	3,629	3,756

Source: AAU, 1991.

Sawyerr notes that, as a result of the ERP/SAP and due to some improvements in the national economy as well as increased donor assistance, government subventions to public universities were increased, leading to improvements in the acquisition of books and other consumables in the universities, the restoration of some confidence and the easing of the brain drain, as evidenced in Table 4 showing staff strength at the University of Ghana.

However, during the 1981–92 PNDC period, enrolments stayed low and stagnant in the face of increasing demand for admission by students and high unit costs per student relative to the share of the national budget devoted to higher education. A general perception of the universities as being too conservative and resistant to the changes being initiated by the PNDC government – due to pressures from the World Bank to institute cost recovery through the removal of student subsidies – culminated in protests leading to university closures in 1987, as well as a period of high tension between the government and the university authorities.

Education sector reforms

The most dramatic change in government-university relations under the PNDC government was the education-sector reforms initiated by the government in 1986 at the behest of the World Bank, which affected all levels of the sector. Before the implementation of the reforms, the structure of the education system was as follows:

- six years of primary education;
- four years of middle school;
- five years of secondary school;
- two years of sixth form, where applicable;

- three years of university (for an honours bachelor degree), although there were some programmes of longer duration, such as Medicine and Architecture.

After the reforms, the structure was changed to:

- six years of primary school;
- three years of junior secondary school;
- three years of senior secondary school;
- four years of university education, although programmes of longer duration, such as Medicine and Law, continued.

The 1991 White Paper (Republic of Ghana, 1991) that led to the above tertiary-level educational reforms had the following objectives:

- expansion in access to tertiary education, including a significant increase in the proportion of female students;
- establishment of a stable and sustainable system of funding;
- reversal of the declining quality of education, and restructuring of enrolment and output in the provision of skills in science, technology, social sciences and humanities in relation to national needs;
- creation of institutional capacities for quality monitoring and policy evaluation in tertiary education.

Sawyerr (1994: 16–17, 20) points out that several aspects of the reform programme had to be negotiated between the Ministry of Education and the university authorities, and implementation of these reforms proceeded slowly in some cases, while certain other provisions were refined. On the other hand, where the reform proposals coincided with measures sought by the universities themselves, they were more readily embraced and implemented. However, there were some instances of resistance, and the phasing-in of some proposals resulted in an improvement of the tertiary reform programme. This was quite different from what occurred with the reform of the pre-tertiary level, where there was little co-ordinated opposition. Once again, Sawyerr credits the internal mechanisms of the universities with rejectng certain aspects of the reform programme and refining others to preserve the minimum conditions considered necessary by the universities to maintain their integrity as institutions of higher learning.

43

As part of the reforms, *higher education* (a term which used to refer only to universities) now became *tertiary education*, encompassing all post-secondary educational institutions, and was placed under the general direction of the Minister for Education. Subsequently, based on the 1992 Constitution of the Republic of Ghana, the erstwhile National Council for Higher Education (NCHE), previously under the Office of the President, was replaced by the National Council for Tertiary Education (NCTE), which served as an advisory body on tertiary education to the Minister for Education. Under this newly revised structure, deputy ministers remained in the Ministry of Education, but tertiary education matters were often not formally assigned to any of the deputies. This situation changed in 2003 when a Minister of State in charge of tertiary education was appointed, ostensibly to give greater attention to matters affecting it. The minister in charge of tertiary education continues to report to the Minister for Education to allow for co-ordination, but it is still too early to judge the effectiveness of this structure.

As a result of these structural changes, the number of candidates seeking admission to tertiary institutions after completing secondary school increased dramatically from about 6,000 to about 20,000 per annum. Together with other factors, this has led to a substantial increase in the number of students registered in tertiary institutions from just under 12,000 in 1990/91 to nearly 54,000 in 2002/3 (see also Table 3 above), resulting in a number of problems for the universities, which are addressed in subsequent chapters.

Akyeampong et al. (1998) and Girdwood (1999) conducted two major reviews of the tertiary education reforms. Leading a review team commissioned by the World Bank and the Ministry of Education, Akyeampong concluded that the eleven objectives of the Tertiary Education Reform Programme (TERP) as set out in the Government White Paper had been only partly attained, due to 'weak monitoring, inadequate planning and poor financing arrangements'. His report then highlighted three key proposals for consideration:

- introduction of fees as a way to improve the precarious financial position of these institutions;

- review of eligibility for student loans. The recommendation was that payment should be based on need as determined, hopefully to reduce the number receiving funds under the scheme;
- selective enrolment policy to ensure that the programmes offered respond to national 'manpower' needs.

Girdwood's (1999) World Bank-commissioned review was to provide an external perspective on the Tertiary Education Reform Programme (TERP). It noted that, although many of the initial policy agreements had not been achieved, considerable progress had been made over the preceding ten-year period within the sector. A number of factors were identified as affecting the mixed results achieved, such as:

- the ability of the government to take the political risks necessary to achieve the desired policy objectives; and
- the weak public sector environment, which hampered the management of effective reform.

In spite of this, Girdwood argued that the institutions themselves might drive the reform process in the future, since progress had occurred in some areas that enhanced their innovative capacity. She identified four key factors as necessary for system management, namely:

- sectoral (and national) planning and budgeting systems, which would provide flexibility for innovation, institutional planning and autonomous decision-making at the lowest level possible;
- sectoral relationships and communication were critical for effective system performance;
- the capacity of the NCTE to play the leading role in guiding and co-ordinating the tertiary education sector and in implementing government policy; and
- awareness and definitions of the principles of autonomy and accountability, noting the importance of striking the right balance between these two principles in order to achieve the desired results.

It is important to note that these reforms were almost entirely dependent on World Bank funds, and therefore a number of the

45

initiatives that would have benefited from funds on a continuing basis were either brought to an end or were severely constrained after its funding ceased. Examples of these were the book and journal subscriptions and the management information system (MIS), which could not be continued in the same manner after the Bank's funding ceased. This is discussed in greater detail in Chapter 7.

Another important educational reform committee completed its work in 2003 – the President's Committee on the Review of Educa- tion Reforms in Ghana chaired by Professor Anamuah-Mensah, Vice Chancellor of the University College of Education, Winneba. Its report, entitled *Meeting the Challenges of Education in the Twenty-First Century* (Republic of Ghana, 2002a), contains observations and recommendations relating to tertiary education. Regarding the struc- ture of tertiary education, the committee recommended that the following institutions should be established to strengthen the educa- tional system in Ghana:

- specialized institutions offering programmes of three years' duration
- an open university offering specific programmes, and
- programmes offered at community colleges.

These new institutions are meant to help address the problems of limited access and inadequate opportunities for academic and professional advancement, in addition to limited opportunities for life-long learning. The report made further recommendations aimed at addressing issues of gender equity, differently able students, private participation in tertiary education and curriculum content and relevance, as well as those relating to the mandates of the various universities. At the time of writing, the government White Paper was still awaited.

Relationships among tertiary sector institutions

Since the tertiary sector now includes institutions other than universities, the issue of collaboration among similar institutions arises, as well as co-operation across types. The law establishing each of these institutions provides a specific mandate, indicating the range of disciplines to be covered in their teaching and research activities. In some instances, there is no overlap in the disciplines covered, which does not facilitate interaction. However, where possible, institutions share resources such as the use of external examiners, part-time lecturers from other institutions, and inter-library lending. There is still room for further collaboration, since a multi-disciplinary approach to many of the issues confronting these institutions is needed. Some of these issues are explored in Chapter 4.

There are also examples of collaboration through affiliation, which usually takes the form of a newer, smaller institution being affiliated to an older, bigger institution. For instance, the University College of Education, Winneba started off as a college of the University of Cape Coast before attaining charter status, while both the Ghana Institute of Journalism and the National Film and Television Institute have affiliate status with the University of Ghana. With the entry of many private universities into the field, the older universities have been processing more applications for affiliation, which serves as a 'mentoring' system for the new institutions. During this period, the NAB has to certify that appropriate standards and quality are maintained. However, the process seems to be only one-way, as it is often assumed that older institutions have nothing or very little to learn from younger ones.

Staff and students in the public institutions interact during staff association activities or student groups. Unfortunately, there is very little interaction at the academic level and few exchanges of students or staff among universities, and it is usually not possible for a student enrolled at one public university to take courses at another. This is in spite of the fact that each of the universities has active student and staff exchange facilities with universities from the United States and Europe. This is further evidence of the extroversion of Ghanaian universities that often emphasize relations with Western counterparts at the expense of co-operation with others within the country, the sub-region or the continent.

At the formal level, Vice-Chancellors, Ghana (formerly the Committee of Vice-Chancellors and Principals) serves as a forum for discussing matters of common interest, so far as the publicly funded universities are concerned. It is possible that, once the private universities are firmly established, such collaboration may be

Box 1 The drift towards the market I: emergence of private universities

The development of private universities in Ghana has proceeded rapidly over the past decade, as a response to the liberalization of the economy and the increasing demand for access. Indeed, the reform of the tertiary education sector emphasized the need to encourage the participation of both the private sector and civil society in the provision of tertiary education. Private providers account for a sizeable share of pre-tertiary education; private schools account for 38.8 per cent of gross enrolment in nursery/kindergarten, 22.4 per cent of primary school education and 14.3 per cent of junior secondary schools. However, they account for smaller shares of senior secondary schools and teacher training colleges; of 510 schools, only 7.1 per cent are privately owned, and only 1 per cent of teacher training colleges are private (MOE/GES, 2002).

As of January 2004, the NAB had accredited 27 private tertiary institutions. Most of these institutions have been established by churches and religious organizations in Ghana and in the diaspora. The NAB requires an institution to affiliate with an existing university for a minimum of four years before it can qualify for charter status. As a result, many of these institutions are affiliated with public universities in Ghana. There are others, however, which are linked with foreign universities such as Wisconsin International University, Ghana and Johns Hopkins University, both from the United States, and the University of KwaZulu-Natal in South Africa.

Currently, the private sector accounts for less than 5 per cent of total enrolment at the tertiary level. However, there are indications that it will continue to grow in terms of the range of programmes offered, as well as the numbers of students enrolled.

A number of features differentiate publicly from privately funded institutions, such as the motivations for their establishment, the types of disciplines covered, the physical location and the size of student numbers. Until recently, the state-instituted and managed student loan scheme did not cover students from private institutions, but it has now been extended to them. There are also pressures to extend to them the benefits of the Ghana Education Trust Fund (GETFund – the government fund introduced in 2001 to fund education), the proceeds of which are derived from a general 2.5 per cent value added tax (VAT) and which, *inter alia*, supports student loans and scholarships.

Private universities typically offer courses in business management, information technology, computing and theological studies. No private institutions offer courses in the sciences as yet, despite policy statements that are biased in favour of science and technology courses. This raises questions about the validity of expressed policy goals to ensure a 60:40 ratio in enrolments in science and arts/social studies respectively. All of the institutions also charge full fees and few of them currently offer reduced fees for skilled but needy or differently able or otherwise marginalized students, raising further questions about equity. While they are likely to expand both their student numbers and their course offerings, private institutions cannot be seen as the answer to the problem of high demand and restricted access to tertiary education in the foreseeable future. There is also a lack in Ghana of sponsorship or scholarship culture that could help students finance private tertiary education. Consequently, private tertiary education is currently an income-based opportunity largely reserved for wealthier groups or classes, which reinforces the elitism of the tertiary system. Another issue is the demand of the private institutions for public funding, without corresponding offers to create schemes to ensure access for broader sections of the population.

expanded, especially as many of them are already affiliated with publicly funded universities. There is a similar body, the Council of Polytechnic Principals, for the polytechnics.

The NCTE is the ultimate body for considering policy matters, mostly relating to funding. For the moment, its activities seem only to cover the publicly funded institutions, but it also exercises some responsibility over private universities through the accreditation process.

While there is little interaction among universities, there is an even lower level of interaction between universities and other tertiary institutions, such as the polytechnics, although it is clear that synergies could be established through common programmes and among faculty in both institutions.

Relationships with other segments of the educational structure

One of the objectives of the tertiary education reforms was to create an environment that ensured that tertiary education was co-ordinated with all other sub-sectors of the educational system and also with overall national policies and priorities. Although all the structures now report to the Minister of Education, there are no formal linkages between the Ghana Education Service Council (responsible for policy matters relating to pre-tertiary education) and the National Council for Tertiary Education (NCTE). Clearly, a formal link would be helpful in the effort to co-ordinate policies between the two sub-sectors, since there is no doubt that developments at the lower levels affect the tertiary level and vice versa.

As it is, the UCC and the UEW relate more with the pre-tertiary sector than do the other three publicly funded universities, because they train teachers for the other levels of the educational system. This is especially true in the area of curriculum development, the design of programmes and research interests. A number of individual university faculty members serve as examiners for relevant subject areas for the West African Examination Council (WAEC), which creates an avenue for interaction at the individual level. This relationship could be formalized to ensure its sustainability beyond the contacts among individuals.

Potential for tertiary education in national development

There is no doubt that tertiary education is essential for national development. As discussed in Chapter 1, following the arguments of Amartya Sen (1999), education in general, and higher education in particular, creates the capabilities needed for people to lead valuable and satisfying lives and to improve their choices, at the same time as the needed skills are imparted. The social opportunities created through education and health care expand the well-being of citizens, while advances in these two areas tend to intensify public demands from all levels of society for innovation in the teaching, learning and research communities represented by universities. In turn, such research and knowledge production influence public policy development and implementation.

In spite of this, several official documents on national development make no reference at all to the sector's contribution. An example is the Ghana Poverty Reduction Strategy, which fails to identify the role of the tertiary education sector directly. This may reflect the failure of the institutions themselves to demonstrate their relevance in such cases, the inability of the appropriate authorities to recognize their importance, or a combination of both. In contrast to the GPRS, the recently completed national ICT policy (Republic of Ghana, 2003b) appropriately acknowledges the roles to be played by the tertiary institutions, among others.

Summing up

This chapter has tried to capture the environment within which public tertiary institutions have developed and operated in Ghana, including their interactions with the government and with each other. As has been shown, the policy environment has not always been conducive to effective academic work and knowledge production, and developments in the national economy have taken their toll on institutional resources. With the deepening of democratic governance, a favourable environment is created for the universities to concentrate on their core mandates. However, there remains the challenge of obtaining the necessary resources to do so in both human and financial terms, a problem that is taken up in Chapter 6.

This chapter has also highlighted the structures within which public universities operate and the way these have improved or impeded the universities' ability to endure pressures from within and without. Another issue is the ability of the public universities to tap into the existing resources of each institution and to create synergies among institutions and throughout the educational sector. These constitute major challenges for the managers of an educational sector in search of change, transformation and a catalytic role in national development.

4 Research & Knowledge Production in Ghanaian Universities

As noted in Chapter 2, universities are sites and systems for knowledge production, and it is in pursuit of this goal that they influence society. Through their teaching and research, new knowledge and refinements of existing knowledge are relayed into teaching, policy and production processes as well as into social life as a whole. In this chapter, we examine the place of research and knowledge production within Ghanaian universities against resources available and demands that undermine the capacity for research, the quality of teaching and the expansion of the system. The following statement by a respondent from the Department of Behavioural Sciences, KNUST, underlines some of the stresses on knowledge production in the universities: 'Research which in the past suffered greatly because of the work-load in teaching and providing community services, has begun to bud and should soon blossom fully'.

To a large extent, the knowledge-producing roles of Ghanaian universities are assumed in their teaching and research functions. Faculty are expected to contribute to knowledge in all their teaching, research and extension activities, which also form the basis for their academic progression. Appointments to professorial grades are made on the basis of recognized contribution to knowledge through scholarly publications at national and international levels. As noted in Chapter 1, loyalty to international norms and standards has often been at the expense of indigenous knowledge systems, which have not been well integrated into university curricula. With notable exceptions, indigenous intellectuals have had no standing or recognition in Ghanaian universities. The inception of a degree programme in herbal medicine at the Faculty of Pharmacy at KNUST (in 2002) is a late recognition of the importance of herbal medicine in the lives of many Ghanaians. Through the Institute of African Studies at the UG and other centres for the study of African and Ghanaian societies, languages and cultures at KNUST and the UCC, space has been found for the scholarly study of indigenous systems in spite of the powerful influence of Eurocentric and Judaeo-Christian perspectives. This is exemplified by the debates over the creation of the University for Development Studies and in its attempt to create

Box 2 The University for Development Studies: a search for difference and relevance

The University for Development Studies was established with the intention of adopting alternative perspectives for teaching, research and community service in a manner reflecting the core mandate of the university. The Faculty for Integrated Development Studies (FIDS) wants to produce graduates well-grounded in the realities of integrated development in poor communities. For this reason, the curriculum seeks to integrate theoretical concepts with extensive field practice in rural communities and districts of Northern Ghana and Brong Ahafo. Similarly, the Faculty of Community Medicine was designed to incorporate the medical needs of the poor into course content responsive to community medical needs. More recently, a Community Nursing Programme was started, in collaboration with the Okanagan University College in Canada.

These 'relevant contexts' and the corresponding course content have been challenged by both students and some faculty, to the point where the medical school feared that it would be producing only 'low-grade medical graduates'. This initially led to the reassignment of students in their third and subsequent years to the 'more established' medical schools at the University of Ghana and KNUST for them to complete their clinical training.

More recently, leadership at the university has re-affirmed its core mandate, thus giving renewed vigour to the idea of a 'development university' exemplified by a third-trimester approach, in which students take regular course work in two trimesters and then devote a third trimester to field practice, placements and community service. Faculty are expected to participate in these activities, which are intended to encourage them to engage in research activities that both enhance their teaching and address the real-life development challenges of poor, rural Ghanaians.

Asked what draws them to the UDS, despite its difficult physical and financial position, students and faculty confirm that:

• the programmes and their community orientation make it possible for students to engage directly with local government institutions and civil society organizations working to support the development of the four regions;

- faculty are engaged in research with a myriad of development agencies in the regions to design, manage and evaluate development projects and programmes;
- UDS has become directly engaged in the national planning of Northern Ghana's poverty reduction strategies.

A continuing challenge in these efforts involves the development of new institutional systems that support the UDS's core mandate.

faculties that deviate from established standards in other Ghanaian universities, as shown in Box 2.

For the majority of Ghanaians, the knowledge-producing roles of universities are viewed in relation to the problems that they face daily, and debates about universities and the national budget are often framed in these terms. In this context, KNUST is seen as the university that holds the key to Ghana's myriad developmental problems. To a large extent, the university also shares this perception, as evidenced in its institutional profile (see Appendix).

In our discussions with key respondents at KNUST, the failure to transform rural housing and sanitation in Ghana, especially in the villages surrounding the university, was cited as one example of KNUST's failure to achieve its core mandate, not only in training human resources, but also in using communities as laboratories to improve the quality of life for Ghanaians. To be sure, KNUST has managed to transfer some technology to artisans through Technology Transfer Units and the *Suame* magazine in Kumasi, the sprawling peri-urban village where largely illiterate artisans fabricate automobile spare parts and machine tools. However, much more is needed to achieve the massive improvements set out in the conceptual framework in Chapter 1. Participants in focus group discussions at KNUST, particularly among the members of the Teachers' and Educational Workers' Union (TEWU) and the Federation of Universities' Senior Staff Association of Ghana (FUSSAG), emphasized that the university needed to expand its role in housing, rural industries, roads and building research in order to make a

55

stronger impact on living standards as well as on economic output and productivity. In this regard, the relationships that KNUST has established with industry and other research institutes, such as those grouped in the Council for Scientific and Industrial Research (CSIR, see Chapter 3), should be strengthened.

In contrast to both the UDS and KNUST, which have sought to implement their core mandates, the case of the University of Cape Coast presented in Box 3 can be seen as a redefinition of mandate with a drift towards the market, in line with the Ministry of Education's policy and the demands of a liberalized economy.

Box 3 The drift towards the market II: 'market-driven' courses at the UCC

In responding to pressures from declining funding and the increasing student demands for 'relevance' to their employment goals, there has emerged an increased emphasis on 'market-driven' courses, especially among the three older universities of Ghana – the UG, KNUST and the University of Cape Coast. These institutions have undertaken various curriculum-restructuring efforts.

At the University of Cape Coast, the phrase 'market-driven' was the operative term for its curriculum review. This generated criticism from some faculty members about the dominance of the market and the commodification of courses and students. In discussions with faculty and students, grave concern was expressed about problems such as possible discrimination against 'non-marketable' courses, which affect courses, including those in the liberal arts, whose added value to education lies in teaching critical thinking. Interestingly, there were no apparent surveys conducted to find out the demands of the market, and sceptics of the curriculum review process also raised the need to consider other criteria like social needs and national goals. In particular, the concern was raised that education, as a core discipline at the UCC, risked being diminished and vocationalized in an effort to make courses more marketable by renaming them without changing their content.

The policy environment

It is hard to find explicit statements relating to knowledge production in government or university policy statements, beyond the NCTE recommended norms for staff/student ratios and enrolment ratios of 60:40 for science/technology and arts/humanities. To a large extent, the funding crunch in the face of expanding student numbers and the inadequate infrastructure in a liberalized economy have so engaged the attention of both policy-makers and university administrators that the core function of knowledge production is largely taken for granted. The Ministry of Education's Policies and Strategic Plans (Republic of Ghana, Ministry of Education, 2001) for universities outlines the following strategies for academic programmes yielding both public and private gains by contributing to the community's well-being as well as preparing students:

- funding of research in tertiary institutions is to be linked to research quality and relevance, and applied research relevant to industry and economic development is to be encouraged;
- quality is to be assured through regular self-assessment and accreditation exercises conducted by the NAB and the National Board for Professional and Technician Examinations (NABPTEX);
- additional funds will be allocated to support excellent academic programmes, balancing science and technology with social science/humanities programmes in universities as well as in polytechnics;
- training faculty members to enrich their pedagogical skills will be supported;
- programmes to identify labour-market and national needs will be developed;
- higher-level technician training and teaching, particularly in polytechnics, will be improved;
- industrial internships and training for staff and students will be encouraged.

Many of these statements are more expressions of intent than policies. They are not supported by the necessary resources, as shown further in this chapter and in Chapter 6. They also fail to acknowledge other conflicting policy documents such as the GPRS, which actually cuts the share of the budget allocated to tertiary

57

education (Republic of Ghana, 2003a). While the NAB was established to encourage high quality academic work in tertiary-level educational institutions, it has not yet had any appreciable impact on the norms and standards of the public universities.

For their part, the universities have attempted to translate some of the policy objectives of the Ministry of Education to their strategic plans. The University of Ghana adopted the following mission statement: 'Our mission is to develop world-class human resources and capabilities to meet national development needs and global challenges, through quality learning, research and knowledge dissemination' (UG, 2001), while the UCC strategic plan (UCC, 2000) notes the challenge of 'promoting research to enhance aspects of local and national socio-economic development'. Similarly, the mission of KNUST is 'to provide an environment for teaching, research and entrepreneurship training in science and technology for the industrial and socio-economic development of Ghana and Africa' (KNUST, 2001) It has grouped fifteen objectives into six themes for the plan period (2001–10). Among the university's immediate priorities are:

- the provision of well-equipped and larger classrooms, lecture theatres, laboratories and studios and well-stocked libraries both to meet the demands of a rising student population and to enhance teaching and learning;
- the recruitment of well-qualified young academic staff to cope with the increase in the student population, by developing outreach programmes and undertaking problem-solving consultancies.

Under the theme of 'Teaching and Research in Science and Technology for Development', KNUST aims to:

- attract, develop, motivate and retain high calibre staff;
- improve the quality of teaching and research;
- expand postgraduate training to promote teaching, research and entrepreneurship training;
- initiate new programmes and undertake research to address the problems of industry and rural communities in response to national needs;
- encourage collaborative research with industry and the private

58

sector and develop stronger collaborative links with other institutions of higher learning and research;
• encourage multi-disciplinary research programmes in the university.

However, resource limitations over the years have put considerable pressure on this sector and thus obstructed the maintenance of high quality academic standards, which suffer from inadequate physical and academic infrastructure and poor conditions of service. The *Report of the President's Committee on the Review of Education Reforms in Ghana* notes that inadequate funding and lack of modern facilities for research, the growing teaching load on faculty due to an increasing number of students, lack of clearly articulated research priorities at the national and institutional levels, absence of strong academic and research leadership and an inadequate number of well-motivated staff at the professional level have all hampered the process of knowledge production at the public universities (Republic of Ghana, 2002a: xxxix).

Research programmes in the universities

The importance of research in universities cannot be overemphasized, as it is research that distinguishes them from other tertiary-level institutions. In many of these universities, research institutes and centres attached to faculties have been established. At KNUST, alongside the research programmes of the organized research units in the Department of Housing and Planning Research (DHPR), the Bureau of Integrated Rural Development (BIRD), the Dairy/Beef Cattle Research Station, the Kumasi Centre for Collaborative Research in Tropical Medicine (KCCR) and the Land Resources Centre, research activities also take place in the teaching departments.

At the University of Ghana, research institutes include the Institute of African Studies, the Institute of Adult Education, the Institute of Statistical, Social and Economic Research (ISSER), the Noguchi Memorial Institute for Medical Research (NMIMR), the Regional Institute of Population Studies (RIPS) and the United Nations Institute for National Resources of Africa (INRA). In addition, many other centres are involved in teaching and research, while many new programmes, usually with external funding, have been established to address the need for development-related research and teaching. The University of Ghana has also been funded by the Carnegie Corporation of New York to establish a learning resources and faculty development centre to improve teaching and research skills for its academic staff, administrative staff and partner institutions.

Currently, much of the research that occurs in the public universities is contract research for organizations. However, in pockets around the universities, there are large funded research programmes, often through joint arrangements with universities and research centres in Europe and the United States. For example, the UG is part of a consortium of four African universities and the London School of Hygiene and Tropical Medicine funded with a $40 million grant from the Bill and Melinda Gates Foundation for the treatment and control of malaria. Research centres at the university – including ISSER, the Institute of African Studies and the Volta Basin Research project – have several large funded research projects.

At KNUST, research units such as the Department of Housing and Planning Research (DHPR), the Bureau of Integrated Rural Development (BIRD), the Dairy/Beef Cattle Research Station, the Kumasi Centre for Collaborative Research in Tropical Medicine (KCCR) and the Land Resources Centre undertake some research in collaboration with foreign partners. Research on the characteristics of harmattan dust particles is being conducted under a co-operative agreement between KNUST and the University of the South Toulon-VAR (UTV) in France. The German Academic Exchange Programme (DAAD) has also sponsored research on the cooling system of rPV modules.

Research and development work are core activities for universities in developing countries such as Ghana, and should make a dynamic contribution to efforts at poverty eradication. In their strategic plans, the universities are giving increased emphasis to applied research. The KNUST plan prioritizes the creation of new programmes and research to address problems in industry and rural communities related to national needs; to encourage collaborative research with industry and the private sector; to develop and strengthen co-operative links with other institutions of higher learning and research; and to encourage multi-disciplinary research programmes in the university. A key thrust of the University of Ghana's strategic plan is 'the re-orientation of teaching, research and extension activities and the harmonization of synergies among disciplines to achieve operational excellence' (UG, 2001).

In line with this mission statement, a School for Research and Graduate Studies has now been established at UG in order to strengthen the synergies between research, teaching, extension and graduate studies. The University of Ghana seeks to upscale its graduate programmes and links with industry, the state and civil society through its research activities. The university intends to achieve this through:

- developing and building a research park
- establishing a consultancy liaison office near the seat of government in Accra
- enhancing graduate fellowships and developing a graduate resource centre
- formulating a training programme in research proposal writing and research skills, and
- promoting North-South and South-South co-operation in graduate training and research.

From the above, it is clear that there is a vital need for all Ghanaian universities to adopt explicit policies to promote and fund more basic research.

University spending on knowledge production

Table 5 shows spending on knowledge production at KNUST, as represented by allocations to research units and the library, which together form only 4 per cent of its ongoing total expenditures. This figure is considerably reduced when personnel emoluments are deducted, calling into question some of the high hopes for research and its potential role in national development outlined above.

A study of expenditures and revenues of tertiary institutions between 1996 and 2000 notes that research funding is not well-defined in the universities, resulting in *ad hoc* allocations of resources to research (Adu and Opoku-Afriyie 2002). The study indicates that, during the five-year period, the percentage of total expenditure attributed to research averaged 2.7 per cent and that these expenditures related mostly to organized research units and not to research performed and funded within specialized academic departments.

61

Table 5: KNUST recurrent budget: allocations by activities, 2001

Cost centre	Year 2001 Actual			
	Personnel emoluments Cedis m.	Goods & services Cedis m.	Total Cedis m.	% of Total Cedis m.
Direct academic expenses				
a) Faculties	21,753.74	7,401.70	29,155.45	56
b) Research units	901.45	753.03	1,654.48	3
General education expenses	2,220.00	3,394.36	5,614.36	11
Library	585.83	64.77	650.60	1
Central administration	2,678.65	668.29	3,346.95	6
Staff/student facilities and amenities	3,703.96	2,399.81	6,103.77	12
Municipal services	3,026.91	294.24	3,321.16	6
Miscellaneous expenses	800.00	1,425.00	2,225.00	4

Source: KNUST, 2002b: 18.

These inadequate funding levels have meant that academic staff must rely on external sources to fund their research projects. The study adds that the NCTE has been unable to define or establish norms for research funding in tertiary institutions.

Typically, university research and conference committees allocate most of their meagre research funding to conference travel rather than to actual research projects. Furthermore, there are few private sector organizations supporting basic research in the universities, although some continue to provide dwindling support to graduate students and programmes.

Attempts to estimate the total research funding given to universities have not been easy, as different offices exist within universities to handle the various funds. Thus, while in the University of Ghana's 2002 financial statements research and awards funds totalled 5.1 billion cedis, a massive increase over the 1.7 billion cedis recorded for 2001, these did not include funds from external sources through the External Funds Office in the School of Graduate Studies and Research (UG, 2002b). The wide variety of arrangements for handling research funds calls for an integrated financial management system to make such figures readily available for planning within and outside the university system.

In addition to financial resources for research, staff quality, which is discussed more fully in Chapter 6, is essential. There is currently an academic staff vacancy rate of 40 per cent in universities, which should be filled by a new generation of lecturers and researchers, whose postgraduate training is examined in the next section.

Ensuring research capacity

The place of postgraduate training

In a recent study of postgraduate education in Ghana, Gyekye (2002:5) notes that the purpose of postgraduate education is the advancement of the intellect and the acquisition of stronger analytical tools and credentials. This endeavour is the proper responsibility of the university boards of graduate studies. At UCC, there are over 30 postgraduate programmes in the Faculties of Science, Agriculture, Arts, Social Science and Education, while at KNUST, there are over 36 postgraduate programmes in the Faculties of Science, Agriculture, Environmental and Development Studies, Pharmacy, and Social Sciences, plus the College of Art, Schools of Engineering and Medical Sciences and the Institutes of Renewable Natural Resources and Mining and Mineral Engineering. The University of Ghana also runs over 45 graduate programmes in the Faculties of Science, Agriculture, Arts, Social Studies, Law and the School of Administration.

Currently, postgraduates make up 8.5 per cent of students at the University of Ghana, compared with 6 per cent at UCC and 7 per cent at KNUST. These figures may be compared with the corresponding figures in their strategic plans: both the University of Ghana and KNUST envisaged 20 per cent postgraduate students,

63

while UCC aimed at 10 per cent postgraduates. Evidently, the universities have not implemented their strategic-plan visions of postgraduate education.

Overall, one-third of students who applied for postgraduate studies over the period 1990–2000 were admitted. At UCC, 55 per cent of applicants are admitted for postgraduate programmes but enrolment figures are invariably less than admissions because some applicants receive offers from more than one university.

As with research, it is hard to determine the share of university budgets earmarked for postgraduate education because of the inadequate funding for universities as a whole. Departments are given sums based on their share of academic-facility user fees for all students, with no specific amount earmarked for graduate training. Gyekye (2002) observes that the cost of postgraduate education cannot be definitely known, apart from bursaries paid by the government and fellowships awarded to some postgraduate students. However, according to him, the cost of producing a Ph.D. graduate in three universities with postgraduate programmes has been estimated as follows:

- Science: 24 million cedis (roughly US$ 2,667) a year;
- Humanities: 20 million cedis (US$ 2,222) a year;
- Engineering: 26 million cedis (US$ 2,888) a year;
- Education: 20 million cedis (US$ 2,222) a year;
- Pharmacy: 30 million cedis (US$ 3,333) a year'
- Medicine: 40 million cedis (US$ 4,444) a year.[7]

While these costs to produce a Ph.D. may be considered high in view of the prevalence of poverty and low per capita incomes in Ghana, they have to be weighed against the potential gains of having Ph.D. graduates in research institutions and other venues where they become producers of new ideas. Gyekye (2002) observes that Ph.D. graduates usually become professors, except for a few very talented individuals without Ph.Ds. Ph.D. graduates also seem more able to do research and publish than masters' degree holders, so they are promoted more quickly. In 2000/1, 54.1 per cent of teaching

[7] The difficulty of estimating these costs is illustrated by the fact that another study put the cost of postgraduate medical education at 63 million cedis or US$7,000 a year (cited in Gyekye, 2002).

Table 6: KNUST postgraduate degrees by faculty/school and gender, 1998–2000

Faculty	1998			1999			2000		
	Male	Female	Total	Male	Female	Total	Male	Female	Total
Agriculture	8	2	10	11	1	12	12	1	13
Art	39	10	49	8	4	12	4	1	5
Engineering	4	0	4	10	0	10	2	0	2
FEDS	49	15	64	56	17	73	65	7	72
SMS	3	0	3	32	5	37	15	1	16
IMME	15	0	15	10	0	10	1	0	1
Pharmacy	3	0	3	3	0	3	2	4	6
Science	21	3	24	25	1	26	16	1	17
Social Science	18	5	23	18	3	21	12	4	16
IRNR	8	0	8	11	1	12	5	1	6
WUC, Tarkwa	10	0	10	0	0	0	0	0	0
ILMAD	0	0	0	0	0	0	0	0	0
Total	178	35	213	184	32	216	132	20	154

FEDS   Faculty of Environment and Development Studies   SMS   School of Medical Sciences
IMME   Institute of Mining and Mineral Engineering   IRNR   Institute of Renewable Natural Resources
ILMAD Institute of Land Management and Development   WUC   Western University College

Note: The figures are for Postgraduate Diploma, M.Sc., MA, M.Phil. and Ph.D candidates.
Source: Extracted from KNUST, 2002a.

and research staff at the University of Ghana possessed doctorates; 33.9 per cent had masters' degrees, while 12 per cent had other qualifications. In the administrative and professional grades, 4.6 per cent had doctorates, 54.3 per cent had masters' degrees, and 41 per cent had other qualifications. The Department of Geography and Resource Development at the University of Ghana, which has perhaps the most Ph.D.s and professors per capita, provides a good illustration of the relationship between Ph.Ds and academic advancement.

Table 6 shows postgraduate degrees awarded by KNUST in 1998–2000. It does not show completion rates, as graduates in a particular year may comprise students who entered at different times. Issues of funding and supervision for graduate students may impede their progress, in addition to delays in the examination of theses arising from the use of both internal and external examiners. On the issue of quality as opposed to the rate of completion, examiners have commented on the antiquated knowledge of some candidates due to the paucity of current books and journals in university libraries, while Gyekye (2002: 25) expresses the opinion that some of the theses produced are not of publishable quality.

To develop a culture of research and performance, Gyekye (2002) advocates enhancing the visibility of graduate programmes through a number of measures. He calls on the boards of graduate studies in the three universities with such graduate programmes to issue a joint annual report listing the titles of all completed theses and dissertations, and indicating where they can be found and to send it to as many university libraries as possible. With advances in ICTs, this could also be done electronically, to save costs and ensure wider dissemination. However, his recommendation entails a level of co-operation among these universities on such matters that does not exist at present, but which could be facilitated by the VCG, NCTE and the Association of African Universities (AAU). There is also a need to improve the instructional skills and research capabilities of lecturers and postgraduate students through more workshops and conferences. Faculty teaching and learning resources centres as well as research and conference committees also have a role to play in this endeavour. The use of sandwich[8] or split-site programmes for postgraduate students is also advocated to broaden their outlook while ensuring that many of them will return to their home institutions and countries. Finally, Gyekye calls on universities to make postgraduate education a separate and autonomous cost centre within the institutions.

Networks and research collaboration

In addition to postgraduate training, universities need to develop collaborative research projects with each other and with other research entities. There are few instances of such co-operation among universities in Ghana and even fewer examples of collaboration with other universities in Africa, except when they are linked by foreign partners.

Other non-university research institutes exist in Ghana. For example, as noted in Chapter 3, the CSIR is a large body devoted to research. Gyekye (2002) endorses closer collaboration between the

---

[8] Programmes, generally undertaken at universities abroad, where teaching staff complete advanced degrees, usually a semester at a time, while retaining their home university positions.

universities and the CSIR, which links 13 research institutes – nine in Accra and four in Kumasi. Within these institutes, there are 101 scientific researchers with doctorates, and 217 with M.Phil. or M.Sc. degrees. CSIR staff are engaged mainly in research, while a few also teach. There is some current collaboration between the CSIR, the UG and KNUST. At KNUST, some staff from CSIR institutes, namely the Crop Research, Soil Science, Forestry Research and Building and Roads Research Institutes (all in Kumasi) teach and supervise postgraduate students on a part-time basis. In the past, science postgraduate students at the University of Ghana did some of their research at CSIR under the supervision of its research staff. Given the dearth of resources at both the universities and the CSIR, greater synergies could be obtained from more vigorous joint efforts.

In addition, some public institutions – such as the Bank of Ghana and the Association of Ghanaian Industries – have research departments, but there appears to be little collaboration with the universities; this is a further resource that could be exploited to share resources including equipment, networking facilities and staff (Gyekye, 2002). Such local arrangements would complement those with foreign partners and could lead to better co-ordination of time and resources. At all the universities visited, it was considered important that many joint agreements were in place or being developed with foreign partners. At KNUST for example, 27 joint agreements with Chinese, Canadian, German, British and American universities and colleges were itemized.

A recent study of the contacts of University of Ghana staff (Garbe, 2004) found that networks are strategic to securing access to important resources, and that particular departments and individuals within the university have used these to their advantage. However, gender affects the networking activities of lecturers, in that female faculty did not have as extensive networks as males because of male dominance in the institutions and the females' tighter time and family constraints. The study also found that budget constraints at the university have made these networks increasingly dependent on external funding, which has led to a trend towards greater networking with European and North American universities than with those in Africa, in spite of its undoubted benefits to African scholarship. Colleagues were seen as a resource for sharing networks. The uneven distribution of computers and Internet access at universities (discussed in Chapter 7) limits their use by many lecturers. The time required in maintaining networks and the time burdens on lecturers arising from large teaching loads and other heavy commitments do not facilitate this sort of networking by most university faculty. Recommendations from the study are:

- that universities should make regional networks a priority in their strategic plans, both for scholars and to promote training;
- that more inter-disciplinary collaboration should be encouraged, along with improved information and communication technology on campus, to facilitate lecturers' networking and enhance their competitiveness;
- that universities consider reducing admissions by about 40 per cent to give lecturers more time for teaching, preparation and research;
- that cost-recovery and cost-sharing could improve universities' income and contribute to better remuneration and research funding;
- that GetFund should allocate more funding for research (Garbe, 2004).

Relationships with other research institutions

There are a number of research institutions that function outside the co-ordination of the Ministry of Education. The most conspicuous of these is the CSIR, which by the nature of its mandate focuses on applied research and therefore could serve as a useful partner to the universities in meeting the needs of society. Even though individuals in the various institutions relate to colleagues in their professional roles, there is no formal link between the universities and these research institutions. Such collaboration would therefore syner-gistically benefit both types of institution.

Ghana Academy of Arts and Sciences (GAAS)

The Ghana Academy of Arts and Sciences is devoted to the advance-ment of knowledge and research, although it does not train students. It is an organization that could meaningfully collaborate with the universities for the advancement of knowledge.

GAAS was established in 1959 as the Ghana Academy of

Learning with the main aim of promoting the 'creation, acquisition, dissemination and utilization of knowledge for national development through the promotion of learning' (*Daily Graphic*, 19 November 2003; see also GAAS, 1981) The criteria for the election of fellows to the academy have been such that the majority have come from universities and research institutions. The academy is now attempting to amend its procedures to invite those outside academia who have made substantial contributions to join as GAAS Fellows. There is also an attempt to broaden the ranks of the disciplines represented. The main activities of the academy are public lectures and seminars, along with the publication of research findings of public interest.

This institution is strategically placed to play a significant role in collaborating with the universities, as it is national in character and also multi-disciplinary. However, most of its activities and its prominent fellows are based in Accra, and it needs to extend its activities beyond Accra for greater impact.

Knowledge production and research centres outside the universities

An unintended offshoot of liberalization in Ghana and throughout Africa has been the emergence of other non-university research centres. These centres – such as the Centre for Policy Analysis (CEPA), the Institute of Economic Affairs (IEA), the African Security Dialogue and Research (ASDR), the Ghana Centre for Democratic Development (CDD), the Third World Network (TWN), the Media Foundation for West Africa (MFWA) and the Institute for Democratic Governance (IDEG), among others are mainly engaged in policy research and advocacy in areas of economic policy, governance, conflict and security. Staff largely comprise former, current or potential university faculty. While most of these centres are located in Accra, with proximity to government and funding agencies and their associated consulting opportunities, they reflect a growing dispersion of knowledge formerly produced in universities. Such centres, funded mainly from grants and consultancy work, pay higher salaries and offer better working conditions than the universities, thus attracting qualified staff away from the universities. University administrators and heads of department feel powerless to prevent this 'brain drain', for fear of losing some of their staff permanently. Some of the research funds that might have gone to the universities have flowed instead to these organizations, some of which have high profiles and work in relevant policy areas, thus depriving universities of both human and financial resources. The existence of these research centres also frustrates universities' attempts to become 'more relevant' or applied.

To date, none of the universities has offered any of these centres an institutional presence within their campuses to pursue their work, in spite of the mutual benefits that such an affiliation would allow: students and other staff might benefit from internships and other work-study opportunities to engage in policy work, while staff of the centres could take advantage of available academic resources, enhancing the value of both endeavours. For this to occur, however, the universities must show more flexibility in their institutional arrangements and their hitherto unchallenged dominance of know-ledge production.

Universities & policy engagement

A growing area of innovation in Ghana has been the emergence on the policy scene of existing or new institutes or centres at universities. Two such institutions, both at the University of Ghana, are particularly worthy of note in this regard.

The ISSER has established a reputation for its annual report on the 'State of the Ghanaian Economy' which collates, verifies and analyzes data on a number of economic indicators. The publication of the results receives national attention and support from academics, the government, non-governmental organizations and donors, and the report serves as an important source of current planning data on Ghanaian economic and social trends.

The Centre for Social Policy Studies (CSPS), also at the University of Ghana, brings academics and social policy practitioners together to share research findings and establish networks for policy advocacy. Parliamentarians, government officials, representatives of civil society and donors have used the centre to frame and develop policy issues, while the centre also incorporates such results into new research initiatives.

Furthermore, the University of Education, Winneba (UEW) has established the Centre for Education Policy Analysis and Studies, which seeks to analyze educational policy issues in Ghana and to establish a related data bank for use by government policy-makers. The centre further seeks to become a centre of excellence by promoting educational research in Ghana and throughout Africa.

The main objectives of this centre are to:

- expand the UEW's capacity to contribute meaningfully to educational development in Ghana;
- assist the School Management Committee and other educational administrators in the proper management of their institutions at all educational levels;
- investigate the effects of current policies on education at all educational institutions and offer recommendations to government thereon;
- establish mutually beneficial links with higher institutions engaged in teacher education in Ghana and abroad.

These objectives are to be realized through contract research for the government and other interested bodies, along with the organization of periodic seminars and workshops for relevant educational groups and the publication of research findings in a quarterly bulletin, *EDUCALERT*.

The opportunity for universities to contribute to Ghanaian public policy-making has always been under-utilized. A major challenge for Ghanaian universities arises with the emergence of think-tanks that attract university staff. The Centre for Economic Policy Analysis (CEPA), the Institute of Economic Affairs (IEA) and the Ghana Centre for Democracy and Development (CDD) are all new public policy institutes that depend on staff from the University of Ghana. Located outside the university, these think-tanks are quasi-consultancies that directly provide services to the public policy process, often through donor-financed events, seminars, workshops and short analytical studies. Their outputs are rarely linked to the teaching, research and learning within the universities, even when their staff hold university positions. By contrast, CSPS at the University of Ghana has developed substantial synergy with the university, by incorporating public policy findings into university teaching.

71

Quality assurance measures

The challenge of knowledge production has both quantitative and qualitative aspects. In the universities studied, there were varying degrees of emphasis on quality assurance systems and practices. The system of external assessment applied in staff recruitment and promotion and the use of external examination in graduate work ensure that staff and students continue to meet internationally recognized standards, while the provision of adequate libraries seeks to support these efforts. To ensure high standards of teaching, there must be highly qualified staff with opportunities for continuing education.

The expansion in access to university education – without a commensurate growth in staffing, infrastructure, facilities, access to international databases and spending on students – has led to major concerns over its quality. There is a growing perception that graduates of the publicly funded universities do not meet either local needs or global standards. In major newspapers around Ghana, these perceptions have led to alarmist headlines about the quality of Ghanaian university graduates; in 2001, a headline in one newspaper read 'Ghanaian University Degrees No Longer Accepted in the UK!'. Along the same lines, it was reported that Unilever Ghana Ltd, a major employer in the private sector, was recruiting graduates from abroad at considerable cost because of the poor performance of recent Ghanaian graduates.

These perceptions contrast sharply with the image that Ghana has built for itself over the years of providing a solid core of graduates who performed well not only in Ghana, but in many international organizations and major corporations. For many Ghanaian universities, the achievements of alumni such as Kenneth Dadzie at the United Nations Conference on Trade and Development (UNCTAD), Mary Chinery-Hesse at the International Labour Organization and Kofi Annan at the United Nations are testimony to the best in Ghanaian higher education. Consequently, reform efforts have focused on the issue of the quality both of staff and of the services provided by the universities. In Chapter 8 below, we examine services and the attempts to improve them.

Quality Assurance Units

An impetus addressing issues of quality followed recent student unrest arising from the introduction of new grading systems in some tertiary institutions. At the UCC, this led to negotiations with the student leadership, resulting in the establishment of mutual systems for evaluating the facilities and the performance of lecturers, and a quality assurance unit aimed at continuous assessment of curricula and faculty.

The UEW has instituted long-standing mechanisms for quality assurance of the teaching, learning and research that are intrinsic to the developmental aspect of its mandate. The College of Health Sciences of the University of Ghana has set up a quality assurance unit concerned with the evaluation of all courses and teachers. The unit offers support for effective teaching and research methods and grant-proposal as well as thesis-writing and note-taking for students and a learning resource centre under the college librarian that promotes students' use of computers.

The University of Ghana is currently evaluating its teaching, learning, research and extension programmes. Course and faculty evaluation systems have been established in some departments and faculties to assist in monitoring teaching effectiveness. The university's strategic plan also proposed a teaching and learning resources centre, which has now been established, as a means of introducing new instructional methodologies for more effective teaching.

Other needed quality assurance measures include graduate tracer studies; opportunities for internship and practical training for students; periodic reviews of university courses and programmes for content and methods; and access to up-to-date information.

The role of libraries

An important dimension of quality in universities is the role of libraries and other resources for teaching, learning and connecting to other scholarly communities. A commissioned study on Ghanaian university libraries reflected the problems resulting from inadequate resources; crippling foreign-exchange difficulties that limit acquisitions; extreme dependence on donors; and libraries' chronic inability to share resources in a resource-starved environment, due to the lack of procedures for resource sharing and inadequate technological infrastructure (Kisiedu, 2002).

According to national norms, libraries should be allocated 10 per cent of the university's recurrent budget, but this has not been

Table 7: Library costs as a percentage of total university expenditures, 1996–2000

Institution	1996	1997	1998	1999	2000
Universities	2.6	2.2	2.0	2.1	2.5
Polytechnics	4.2	4.1	2.5	3.8	3.9
Norm	10	10	10	10	10

Source: Adu and Opoku-Arfiyie, 2002.

achieved; the average library budgets have ranged between 2 and 4 per cent. Table 7 shows university expenditure on libraries between 1996 and 2000.

The introduction of an academic facility user fee, under which 10-15 per cent of receipts are allocated to libraries, has allowed some libraries to make local acquisitions. In addition, other libraries have received infrastructure development funding from GETFund. Nevertheless, major library projects have been undertaken mostly through the assistance of foreign donors such as the World Bank and the Danish International Development Agency (DANIDA).

Kisiedu's study on libraries conducted as part of the universities' case study showed all library heads expressing profound concern about the small size of their collections and the paucity of resources for acquisitions. The total stock of university libraries is low, at about 900,000 volumes in both main and specialized libraries. The weakest collection area is in current journals, with the UDS and the UEW lacking any serial subscriptions at all at the time of our visits to them in 2001–2. This does not allow Ghanaian libraries to provide any information support in areas in need of current materials, such as medical and health sciences, environmental studies, engineering and applied science and technology.

While individual projects have provided funding for the libraries, they also raise sustainability issues. As Kisiedu notes, the World Bank's 1985-2000 project to support textbooks and journals temporarily improved the situation of many libraries to some extent – each participant library received several hundred thousand dollars for books, journals, electronic equipment and staff training – but when the project came to an end, the libraries once again faced a situation of inadequate funding.

74

Currently, the libraries are implementing the Programme for the Enhancement of Research Information (PERI) project, organized by the International Network on the Availability of Scientific Publications, under which they can select print journal subscriptions. Kisiedu warns, however, that when the programme expires in 2006, without replacement funding, these libraries will be left with increasingly outdated back files with no current issues, as de Bruijn and Robertson (1997) noted with respect to the World Bank project.

Except for the UCC, which has recently expanded its campus buildings, the universities also complained of inadequate space for collections and reading.

However, there are some areas of hope, particularly in technological infrastructure development, networking and resource sharing, which are discussed further in Chapter 7. Local funding is also receiving attention at institutional and national levels. In the recent strategic plans of universities, some attention is given to the need for better library infrastructure.

Publications

The quality of its research and publications is the hallmark of any university. In Ghana, many university journals stopped publication during the late 1970s as the economic crisis deepened. In recent years, some of these abandoned journals have been revived, and some of the backlog at Ghana Universities Press from the late 1970s and 1980s has now been published, while many existing books have been reprinted to meet the needs of more students. While textbooks in many disciplines are still imported, many more staff publications in the social and natural sciences, arts and law are available in university bookshops.

However, there is no organized compilation of university publications in Ghana. The universities need to report more fully on their knowledge-producing activities. The use of university websites to list publications and research would improve their visibility and offer reliable information. The production of citation indices and other tools to track the use of publications by Ghanaian scholars in Ghana would strengthen the local and international reputation of Ghanaian universities. Systematic use of ICTs to list and publish journals and books is another avenue that would reduce costs, reach a broad audience and prevent the one-copy-one-user problem, with the potential to generate income when publications are placed in international academic databases.

Gyekye (2002) notes that only a few of the theses produced by graduate students in the public universities are eventually published as books. However, some chapters are subsequently published in books and journals. Thanks to the AAU, thesis abstracts from African universities will soon be available online through the Database of African Theses and Dissertations (DATAD) project. It is hoped that this initiative will be sustained through the universities' departments of information studies and will also help to select the better ones for publication.

Most academic publishing in Ghana is done through the Ghana Universities Press (GUP), established in 1962 to publish scholarly work. Originally funded by the government, it became a commercial unit in November 2002 under the Subvented Agencies Reform Programme of the National Institutional Renewal Programme. Nevertheless, its functions have not been compromised; it still publishes for the universities, mainly the University of Ghana and the University of Cape Coast, which also contribute most of the material.

Before 1985, the GUP published about six titles a year, in addition to inaugural and occasional lectures. By 1988, close to 20 titles were being published yearly, which may be linked to the growth in university faculty numbers before the 1987 reform programme. Since the early 1990s, publications have picked up again, and up to ten titles are now published per annum. Usually 1000 copies are printed initially, with reprints based on demand.

Two to three of the ten annual titles produced on average are textbooks, suggesting an interesting trend. According to the GUP manager, before 2000 many scholarly publications were not attuned to course work. However, this is changing now, and the press is encouraging faculty members to publish more textbooks in response to market needs. Since the GUP lacks funds to commission publications, it approaches potential authors with offers of editorial assistance. The increase in student enrolments has also improved textbook sales. The social sciences have more students and therewith more publications: some sociology books by University of Ghana faculty have been reprinted three times and have gone into new editions. In contrast, there are few titles in the sciences, while publications in education have remained popular and widely used,

76

especially by students from the UCC and UEW, as well as in the teacher training colleges.

The GUP is also involved in the Ministry of Education's schools textbook programme, with particular responsibility for maths and science books. In this significant market, print runs are often over 50,000 copies, and these are sold to the ministry. These books are mostly produced by university lecturers.

The press manager is optimistic about the GUP's future prospects, with the rapid expansion in student numbers supporting a growing market. The teaching of theology in many private universities offers another publishing opportunity for the GUP, which intends to recruit faculty from the departments of religion in the public universities to produce texts in this area.

As a result of liberalization and increased print resources, many private presses also offer outlets for faculty publication. Some of these presses, including Woeli Publishing Services, Sub-Saharan Publishers and older publishers such as Afram Publications, have published many academic titles, and book launches have now become a regular feature of the Ghanaian cultural scene.

Although the GUP publishes some university journals, other journals are produced independently. The University of Cape Coast publishes the following faculty-based journals:

- *Oguaa Social Science Journal* (JOSS)
- *Asemka* (Faculty of Arts)
- *African Studies Journal*
- *Journal of Natural Science* (Faculty of Science)
- *Ghana Journal of Chemistry* (Department of Chemistry)

Some of these journals have appeared intermittently as a result of funding problems, such as the *African Studies Journal* which has not appeared since its first issue in 1975. Yet others have managed to survive; during 2001/2, *JOSS* and *Asemka* came out with new editions. Some of these journals, including the *Ghana Journal of Chemistry*, serve a much wider constituency than just the universities, and embrace teachers at the secondary and teacher training levels.

Many other journals are produced at the University of Ghana, including *The Legon Journal of Sociology, The University of Ghana Law Journal, The Research Review* (of the Institute of African Studies), *The*

77

Transactions of the Historical Society of Ghana, Legon Social Science Journal, Ghana Journal of Literacy and Adult Education and the *Legon Journal of International Affairs.* With growing Internet access, the Institute of African Studies' *Research Review,* which has remained current since 1985, is available online, under the African Journals Online (AJOL) project. It also has licensing agreements with other distributors to ensure online accessibility. Other journals that have re-emerged after a long hiatus – such as the *Transactions of the Historical Society of Ghana* and *Asemka* – will probably continue production and will soon be available across Africa and in libraries worldwide.

Summary

This chapter has attempted to deal with a number of issues affecting knowledge production and research in Ghanaian universities under conditions of increasing student numbers, inadequate staff and stagnant budgets for research and libraries. It has also explored the role of postgraduate training in expanding research capacity and the collaboration among Ghanaian universities and with other research centres in Ghana and elsewhere in Africa. Universities are called upon to articulate clearer visions of postgraduate education and to set targets and earmark resources for its development, while exploring the use of collaborative programmes to provide broader exposure to students. The place of improved networks, quality assurance units, libraries and publications in facilitating the production and dissemination of knowledge and the challenge of new research and policy centres call for self-examination by the universities and some flexibility to deal with these new opportunities.

5 Ensuring Access with Equity

Articles 25(1) and 38(1) of the 1992 Constitution provide for free, compulsory and basic education as well as equal access to tertiary education, with an emphasis on science and technology. In addition, the White Paper on education also emphasizes the need to significantly increase the proportion of female students to a target of 50 per cent. Key strategies for achieving these objectives are:

- establishing a tertiary system which is both horizontally and vertically integrated with the rest of the education sector so that students enjoy flexibility in their programmes and disciplines;
- setting admissions criteria that ensure adequate resources for each student;
- eliminating possible barriers to participation in tertiary education of qualified students on grounds of poverty, gender, disability, religion, race or ethnicity;
- creating opportunities for working people to participate in tertiary education through distance education and lifelong learning programmes;
- encouraging the participation of the private sector and civil society in tertiary education and the establishment of private tertiary institutions.

Vis-à-vis these objectives, a central preoccupation of university administrators and policy-makers in Ghana has been balancing dwindling facilities in view of the increasing demand. The corresponding increases in enrolment and an apparently decreasing access for a growing section of the population raise an important challenge of rethinking access and equity. The normal approach to opening up access to university education in Ghana has been to increase enrolment through student admissions, the forms of which might be diversified through 'different windows', such as admitting more mature students, establishing external degree centres and strengthening distance education. These strategies have resulted in modest enrolment increases at the five publicly funded universities over the past decade. From a total of 9,997 students in 1990, enrolment increased in all publicly funded universities by an average of 12 per cent per annum to a total of 47,589 students in 2002–3 and 63,576 in 2003/4 (NCTE, 2004).

Enrolment at the UEW doubled in the five years between 1996 and 2001, from 3,500 in 1996 to 7,059 in September 2001, owing in part to the significant emphasis that the university has placed on distance education (UEW, 2002). The University of Development Studies (UDS), has been experiencing increases in enrolment, with the largest increase from 433 in 2001/2 to 888 in 2002/3, an increase of over 100 per cent (UDS, 2002).

Yet, in spite of the publicly advertised minimum requirements for admissions to universities in Ghana, less than 35 per cent of those who apply are admitted, as these admissions continue to become increasingly competitive. According to Professor Addae-Mensah, former Vice-Chancellor of the University of Ghana:

... every year, we are faced with the painful decision of having to reject a large number of highly qualified students. We have now reached, or probably even surpassed, the optimum number of students that our present facilities and staff strength can cope with. Last academic year the total population of the University reached about 14,600. Statistics available to me indicate that our population is over 15,000. In both absolute numbers and percentage increase in enrolment, the University has tried to meet the aspirations of a large number of the qualified students, but the sheer increase in the number of qualified candidates every year is making this a really daunting task (Addae-Mensah, 2001: 47).

Table 8 shows that, for the University of Ghana, less than a third of applicants for admissions in 2001 were actually offered places at the university. This percentage, although registering an increasing

Table 8: Applications and admissions to University of Ghana, 1997–2001

Year	No. applied	No. admitted	No. enrolled	% of total applicants
1997	10,613	3,880	3,000	28.1
1998	12,931	4,322	3,260	25.2
1999	14,319	5,697	4,679	32.7
2000	16,966	6,581	5,237	30.9
2001	18,252	7,912	5,986	32.8

Source: Addae-Mensah, 2001: 37–8.

trend since 1997, also demonstrates the very low proportion of admitted students against applicants, suggesting that the best efforts still fall short of satisfying the demand for university education in the country.

Table 9: Secondary schools contributing 50 per cent or more of students to universities

School	Frequency	%	Cumulative %
Presec	55	3.7	3.7
Prempeh College	48	3.2	6.9
Achimota School	47	3.2	10.1
Wesley Girls High	41	2.8	12.8
St Augustine's College	38	2.6	15.4
Holy Child	38	2.6	17.9
Aburi Girls' Secondary School	32	2.1	20.1
St Roses Secondary	30	2.0	22.1
Accra Academy	29	1.9	24.0
Mfantsipim School	27	1.8	25.8
Tamale Secondary School	27	1.8	27.7
Opoku Ware School	26	1.7	29.4
Pope John Secondary	22	1.5	30.9
Mfantsiman Girls' Secondary School	21	1.4	32.3
Adisadel College	20	1.3	33.6
St Peter's Secondary School	18	1.2	34.8
Mawuli School	17	1.1	36.0
St Louis Secondary School	17	1.1	37.1
Labone Secondary School	17	1.1	38.3
Bishop Herman College	16	1.1	39.3
Ghana Secondary Technical School	16	1.1	40.4
KNUST Secondary School	15	1.0	41.4
Fijai Secondary School	15	1.0	42.4
Ghana National College	15	1.0	43.4
St John Bosco Training College	15	1.0	44.4
Presbyterian Training College	15	1.0	45.4
Tema Secondary School	14	0.9	46.4
St Mary's Secondary School	14	0.9	47.3
Aggrey Memorial Secondary School	14	0.9	48.3
Total	719	48.3	
Overall Total	1490		

Source: Survey conducted as part of the Ghana Universities Case Study, 2002.

81

The increased enrolment figures for Ghana's five publicly funded universities mask distortions in access and equity. Further analysis (see below) shows some inherent disadvantages in access with respect to types and locations of secondary schools, region of origin and students' socio-economic background, and gender.

In a lecture at the Ghana Academy of Arts and Sciences, Addae-Mensah (2000) revealed that, although there are over 600 senior secondary schools producing applicants to Ghanaian universities, more than 75 per cent of those admitted came from only 50 schools. This revelation prompted some discussion in the public media ('Few Schools Contribute Students to Universities', *Daily Graphic*, 31 August 2002). Indeed, the survey of 1,500 students conducted for the present study also suggested a similar trend, with 50 per cent of the students in the five publicly funded universities coming from only 29 schools.

The survey showed that there were wide variations among Ghana's ten regions in gaining admission to university. Over 75 per cent of the students cited five regions – Ashanti, Eastern, Greater Accra, Volta and Central Regions – as their regions of origin, with the Eastern Region having the highest percentage at over 18 per cent. The remaining five regions had extremely low percentages, averaging 4-6 per cent. Interestingly, the three regions of Northern Ghana, considered the poorest in the country, had similar figures to those of Western and Brong Ahafo Regions. Table 10 presents a summary of the regions of origin in the survey of students from the five publicly funded universities.

The most significant factor enhancing the chances of access to university in Ghana was the region (and indeed, location) of residence. Table 11 from the survey of students reveals that nearly 70 per cent of the students in the five universities reside in only three regions, namely, the Greater Accra, Ashanti and Eastern Regions, suggesting that students from these regions have the best chance of gaining entrance to university. Discussions with students confirmed this finding, revealing that many students and parents sought to find relatives in urban areas and regions with better-equipped schools in order to improve students' chances of university admission.

The increases in enrolment have not been matched by corresponding improvements in university facilities. The overall student/staff ratios in 2003 were 27:1 for KNUST, 39:1 for the UCC and 28:1 for the UG, instead of the norm of 15 students to one lecturer (NCTE,

Table 10: Region of origin of selected students by university

Region	KNUST		UCC		UEW		UDS		UG		Total	
	No.	%	No.	%	No.	%	No.	%	No.	%	No.	%
Ashanti	98	24.3	35	12.4	31	15.7	11	11.6	82	16.6	257	17.4
Brong-Ahafo	21	5.2	16	5.7	10	5.1	3	3.2	13	2.6	63	4.3
Central	54	13.4	62	22.0	27	13.6	5	5.3	59	11.9	207	14.1
Eastern	72	17.8	57	20.2	33	16.7	3	3.2	101	20.4	266	18.1
Greater Accra	38	9.4	28	9.9	9	4.5		0.0	54	10.9	129	8.8
Northern	9	2.2	12	4.3	16	8.1	25	26.3	29	5.9	91	6.2
Upper East	9	2.2	7	2.5	12	6.1	26	27.4	18	3.6	72	4.9
Upper West	17	4.2	13	4.6	10	5.1	13	13.7	9	1.8	62	4.2
Volta	65	16.1	31	11.0	41	20.7	6	6.3	101	20.4	244	16.6
Western	17	4.2	21	7.4	9	4.5	3	3.2	18	3.6	68	4.6
Others	4	1.0	0		0		0		10	2.0	14	1.0
Total	404	100	282	100	198	100	95	100	494	100	1473	100

Source: Survey conducted as part of the Ghana universities case study, 2002.

Table 11: Region of residence of selected students by university

Region	KNUST		UCC		UEW		UDS		UG		Total	
	No.	%	No.	%	No.	%	No.	%	No.	%	No.	%
Ashanti	130	32.3	39	14.2	44	22.4	11	11.7	48	9.9	272	19
Brong-Ahafo	8	2.0	12	4.4	16	8.2	6	6.4	12	2.5	54	4
Central	13	3.2	36	13.1	17	8.7		0.0	12	2.5	78	5.6
Eastern	33	8.2	17	6.2	24	12.2		0.0	35	7.2	109	7.3
Greater Accra	160	39.8	107	38.9	39	19.9	16	17.0	305	63.1	627	40
Northern	9	2.2	11	4.0	14	7.1	38	40.4	17	3.5	89	7.7
Upper East	3	0.7	5	1.8	3	1.5	15	16.0	14	2.9	40	3.2
Upper West	10	2.5	6	2.2	7	3.6	4	4.3	3	0.6	30	2.3
Volta	12	3.0	12	4.4	17	8.7		0.0	21	4.3	62	4.2
Western	21	5.2	30	10.9	15	7.7	4	4.3	16	3.3	86	6.2
Others	3	0.7	0.0	0.0	0.0	0.0	3	0.2				
Total	402	100	275	100	196	100	94	100	483	100	1450	100

Source: Ibid.

83

2004). Furthermore, student residence facilities have exceeded recommended occupancy limits by as much as three-fold.

To cope with rising enrolments and inadequate facilities, the universities have had to innovate. At the UEW, some required courses have been delivered through the student-operated FM radio stations. Students are encouraged to stay in their halls of residence for these radio lectures which are interspersed with face-to-face sessions among groups of students, where they are able to ask questions and discuss the material. Adult learners indicated that these study groups allowed slow learners to share insights, formulate questions and generally develop their thoughts in a co-operative rather than a competitive manner. Furthermore, the development of radio learning groups by students and the preparation of radio lectures by faculty also became part of an emerging tradition of innovative teaching and learning methods at the UEW.

A standard response to the space problem has been the construction of new and expanded lecture halls by all the universities in Ghana. The UCC, KNUST, UG, UEW and UDS have been expanding their facilities through multi-purpose lecture halls. The UEW pioneered the use of pavilion lecture theatres with seating capacity for 500 students. These cost much less and were faster to construct than fully covered lecture halls

In terms of residential facilities, the crunch in student housing has led all the universities to increase investment in campus housing. At KNUST, joint financing for housing was developed through a partnership between the Student Representative Council and the university. Universities have also been making efforts to house students in local communities, and several private hostels have been constructed to serve the 61 per cent of students who do not live on campus. The Social Security and National Insurance Trust (SSNIT) recently completed 400-bed hostels in the vicinity of the University of Ghana and at KNUST. Alumni of the University of Ghana also initiated a multi-billion cedi housing complex, known as Jubilee Hall, as their gift to the university in celebration of its golden jubilee. The first phase was opened in September 2002 for some 600 students. When completed, it should provide accommodation, cafeteria, conference and other facilities for over 1000 students.

While construction remains the standard response to the growing demand for facilities, some universities have fabricated different, more innovative strategies for both the mode and the delivery of courses. To cope with increasing numbers, the UEW has restructured its four-year bachelor of education programme so that students spend the first three years on campus, reserving the last year for a teaching internship in Ghanaian schools. Designated as the 'in-in-in-out' programme, the content of the former B.Ed. programme has been compressed into the first three years of the restructured programme to provide a 40-week internship for prospective graduate teachers in place of the former four-week internship period.

There are plans to shorten the course further through an 'in-out-in-out' formula, which would require only a two-year residence for all students at the UEW, with the other two years spent off-campus. Such an arrangement would relieve the constraint on enrolments, while restructuring teaching methods to give graduates more practical teaching and learning experience. Furthermore, lecturers' support for interns in the field would increase, thereby enriching the latter's research methods and real-life educational inputs. In effect, these strategies hold the potential for transforming teaching, learning and research in a university that has that precise mandate.

This pattern of creative solutions is becoming institutionalized at the UEW and other universities. The basic education programme is already being taught at the UEW through distance education, helping many teachers to upgrade their qualifications while they continue teaching. This conforms to the policy of the Ministry of Education to curb flows out of the classroom, which created vacancies that were filled by untrained teachers. According to the Report of the President's Committee on the Review of Education Reforms in Ghana (Republic of Ghana, 2002a) in the 2000/01 academic year there were 19,141 vacancies for teachers at the basic level, of which only 6,285 were filled. Moreover, of the number teaching at that level, 27,398 were untrained (ibid.: 97). There is also a reported attrition rate of about 2,000 teachers per annum.

Distance-education programmes have gained currency in all the universities. The University of Ghana, with its external degree centres, is already reaching thousands of students through the Accra Workers' College, with the potential for expanding these facilities into the other nine regional centres with similar facilities. The UEW also initiated a distance-education programme involving 1,500 teachers for tutors at training colleges to bring them up to degree level. Centres have been established in Winneba, Kumasi, Tamale, Hohoe, Pusiga, Koforidua and Accra. These centres have been developing plans to go electronic, with seed grants from GetFund. It is envisaged that each centre will be equipped with audio-visual facilities, and the main centre in Winneba will have the capacity for video documentation of lectures to be distributed on CD-ROMs.

Equity issues

While these innovations permit higher enrolments, equity issues remain important in the expansion of access. According to the Executive Secretary of the NCTE, the Ghanaian government has agreed to reserve 5 per cent of spaces in the public universities for foreign students, while keeping another 5 per cent of places for fee-paying Ghanaian students. The universities will retain control of the remaining 90 per cent of admissions. Slots for personal sponsorship will remain, combined with strategies to cater for poor and rural

Table 12: UDS student enrolment by year, faculty and gender, 1993–4/2002–3

Year	Faculty												Grand total		
	Agriculture			School of Medical and Health Sciences			Institute of Development Studies			Faculty of Arts and Sciences					
	M	F	Total	M	F	Total	M	F	Total	M	F	Total	M	F	Total
1993/4	39	-	39	-	-	-	-	-	-	-	-	-	39		39
1994/5	36	4	40	-	-	-	53	6	59	-	-	-	89	10	99
1995/6	17	3	20	-	-	-	13	4	17	-	-	-	30	7	37
1996/7	45	1	46	15	8	23	28	8	36	-	-	-	88	17	105
1997/8	69	5	74	29	3	32	51	12	63	-	-	-	149	20	169
1998/9	80	7	87	42	8	50	55	17	72	-	-	-	177	32	209
1999/2000	76	5	81	13	6	19	45	13	58	-	-	-	134	24	158
2000/1	91	11	102	10	3	13	47	18	65	-	-	-	148	32	180
2001/2	150	43	193	42	23	65	130	45	175	-	-	-	322	111	433
2002/3	249	53	312	50	41	91	212	148	360	100	25	125	611	277	888
Total	852	142	994	201	92	293	634	271	905	100	25	125	1,787	530	2,317

Source: UDS, 2002.

students. For some time now, KNUST has been using discretionary criteria to admit students from poor rural areas to highly desirable courses such as medicine and engineering.

At the UDS, radical and holistic strategies for access and equity have been initiated on behalf of students from poor backgrounds and to ensure gender equity. To promote gender equity across all programmes, especially in the sciences, it was decided to admit all female applicants satisfying the basic entry requirements. This decision raised female enrolments in all programmes in the 2002/3 academic year, more than doubling the 111 females in 2001/2 to 277 in the 2002/3, with female enrolment in the School of Medical and Health Sciences coming close to parity at a ratio of five males to four females. Table 12 compares enrolments by sex from 1993/4 to 2002/3 academic years, depicting the decisive impact and success of this programme.

Socio-economic equity

An explicit purpose and mandate of the UDS has been to bring university education to the three regions of Northern Ghana and the Brong Ahafo region, where students have little chance of admission to the older universities. Yet the UDS has also pursued an orthodox admissions policy, with the result that those unable to meet the highly competitive requirements of the older universities select the UDS. These students, from other regions, often gain admission ahead of the best students from the four target regions, whose grades are poorer because of inadequate preparation, whereas the proposed admissions standards for the UDS should enhance access for these disadvantaged students. According to the proposal, all candidates who meet the UDS's basic entry requirements will be ranked by position in their schools of origin; students from similar schools will then compete in their cluster, with the top percentage of each being admitted. Such a strategy, now adopted by the UDS, meets the increasing public demand for a quota system for rural students[10] to improve their access to university education and

[10] 'Call for Quota System for Rural Students', *Daily Graphic*, 11 September 2002: 19. This call was made by Alfred Kofi Appiah, Executive Director of Childrens' Rights International, an NGO advocating educational rights for children, the poor and the vulnerable in society.

thereby redress the imbalance between urban and rural secondary schools.

This system, combined with its gender equity measures, shows how the UDS is addressing critical questions of equity and access, separating these from the traditional focus on means to increase enrolment. Such strategies have many implications for the wider society as well as for university offerings. A gender balance in classes, as exemplified by the impact of the 2002–3 admissions policy in the School of Medical and Health Sciences, could have a profound impact on teaching and general student experience. Similar demographic and gender shifts in other faculties also raise the potential for universities to assist the government in the alleviation of poverty and other social ills.

6 Resource Mobilization & Management

One of the biggest challenges to the management of the public universities has been in putting their human, financial and physical resources to best use in achieving their objectives and targets. A vision can only be realized through the effective harnessing of the appropriate resources to specific objectives, and ensuring their availability in terms of quality, quantity, timeliness and adaptability to changing needs. This chapter seeks to analyze the process of resource development and management by the institutions under consideration.

Human resource management & institutional development

The quality of a university is largely determined by its human resource base: its teaching, research, administrative, professional and other support staff. This has become an increasing concern since the late 1970s. In the 1950s and 1960s, outstanding students with high academic potential were granted scholarships to undertake graduate studies either locally or abroad. In the mid-1980s, this scheme was discontinued partly because of lack of funds and partly due to the high default rate, as many recipients studying overseas did not return. Even though training outside Ghana has not been completely abandoned, it is no longer the main means of training potential academics. For example, departments with strong in-house postgraduate programmes – such as the Departments of Geography at both the University of Ghana and the University of Cape Coast – are still able to recruit staff from among their own postgraduate students. It has also been recognized that the acquisition of a doctorate degree does not automatically *per se* prepare a person to teach effectively. The University of Ghana has therefore set up a centre for faculty development and learning resources in order to assist faculty members to improve their teaching performance.

Staff attraction/retention and turnover

According to the NCTE (NCTE, 2004), staffing norms for the universities require a academic staff/student ratio of 1:12 for

89

Table 13: Student/academic staff ratios and norms for public universities, 2003/2004

Full-time	Student enrolment	No. of staff	Student/staff ratios	NCTE norm
Science	18,726	755	25	12
Medicine	2,013	307	7	8
Pharmacy	602	34	18	12
Humanities	36,009	763	47	18
Education	6,226	76	82	15

Source: NCTE, 2004.

Science; 1:8 for Medicine; 1:18 for Humanities, and 1:15 for Education. Table 13, giving student/staff ratios for 2003/4 shows that all the disciplines except Medicine are grossly understaffed. Pharmacy is not so under-served, but Education has the worst ratio, though this may be due to the fact that some of its faculty in sandwich programmes may not have been converted into full-time equivalents.

Table 14 shows staff numbers by grade at KNUST, revealing huge inadequacies particularly in teaching, research and administration, to the detriment of these areas.

Similarly, while NCTE's national norms stipulate an overall institutional student/staff ratio of 15:1, in 2001/2, there were only 700 academic staff at the University of Ghana, compared with 15,000 students, giving a ratio of about 22:1. The result is large classes without adequate support systems, such as large, well-equipped

Table 14: KNUST staff by grade, March 2002

Category of Staff	Staff in post	Staff required	% of required staff in post
Teachers (lecturers)	473	978	48.3
Research fellows	21	45	46.7
Librarians	10	15	66.7
Senior administrators	77	224	34.3
Technicians/senior staff	553	825	67.0
Junior staff	1,784	2,140	83.4
Total	2,918	4,227	69.0

Source: KNUST, 2002a.

Table 15: Academic staff pyramid by discipline in the public universities, 2003–04

	Professor	%	Senior Lecturer	%	Lecturer	%	Total
Norm		20.0		30.0		50.0	
Science	101	13.4	193	41.9	461	61.1	755
Medicine	54	17.6	88	53.3	165	53.7	307
Pharmacy	5	14.7	10	52.6	19	55.9	34
Humanities	86	13.7	164	43.3	379	60.3	629
Education	14	6.7	37	23.3	159	75.7	210
Total	260	13.4	492	41.6	1,183	61.1	1,935

Source: NCTE, 2004.

lecture rooms and sufficient numbers of graduate teaching assistants. This situation has led the university to suspend undergraduate continuous assessment, which constitutes 30 per cent of the grade, in the Faculties of Arts and Social Studies, where classes tend to be large.

As can be seen from Table 15, the existing proportions vary widely from the expected norm. Only Medicine comes close to the required 20 per cent for the professorial grade. It is also interesting that those disciplines with relatively few senior persons have very high student numbers relative to staff available, raising concerns about quality in the knowledge-production roles of universities and the promotion prospects of staff. Relative to student numbers, the academic staff in Medicine has higher percentages in both professorial and senior lecturer grades, compared with academic staff in the Humanities or Education.

Age structure of faculty

A look at the age structure in the public universities reveals that about 40 per cent of the teaching and research staff are above 50 years of age and will therefore be retiring soon at the compulsory retirement age of 60. Concern about this is reinforced by the survey undertaken by this study, as shown in Table 16. The UDS, the youngest of the five universities, also has the youngest mix of faculty, with over 75 per cent under the age of 45. Conversely, in the two older universities – the University of Ghana and KNUST –

91

Table 16: University faculty by age group

Age groups	KNUST No.	%	UCC No.	%	UEW No.	%	UDS No.	%	UG No.	%	Total No.	%
under 31		0.0		0.0		0.0		0.0	1	1.2	1	0.4
31-35	11	12.9	5	12.8		0.0	5	20.8	4	4.7	25	9.0
36-40	16	18.8	1	2.6	5	11.4	5	20.8	9	10.5	36	12.9
41-45	16	18.8	8	20.5	5	11.4	9	37.5	21	24.4	59	21.2
46-50	18	21.2	9	23.1	13	29.5	3	12.5	14	16.3	57	20.5
51-55	12	14.1	8	20.5	14	31.8	2	8.3	25	29.1	61	21.9
56-60	10	11.8	5	12.8	6	13.6		0.0	7	8.1	28	10.1
60+	2	2.4	3	7.7	1	2.3		0.0	5	5.8	11	4.0
Total	85	100.	39	100	44	100	24	100	86	100	278	100

Source: Faculty Survey conducted as part of the Ghana Case Study, 2002.

Table 17: Age profile of universities' academic staff, (1998/1999)

Universities	30 years or less No.	%	31-40 years No.	%	41-50 years No.	%	51-60 years No.	%	>60 years No.	%	Total Total
UG	0	0.0	88	17.7	236	47.4	119	23.9	55	11.0	498
KNUST	6	1.3	93	19.7	200	42.3	139	29.4	35	7.4	473
UCC	4	1.8	42	18.6	95	41.8	63	27.7	23	10.1	227
UCEW	0	0.0	32	17.6	95	52.2	48	26.4	7	3.8	182
UDS	2	3.0	27	40.3	30	44.8	7	10.4	1	1.5	67
Grand total	12	0.8	282	19.5	656	45.3	376	26.0	121	8.4	1447

Source: NCTE, 2002

between 50 and 60 per cent of staff are aged 46 and older. Consequently, the universities tend to retain retired staff and faculty on contract: an average of 10 per cent of faculty in most of the universities are currently on contract.[11] Some of the factors that affect staff quality assurance, such as ageing and inadequate numbers, were also addressed in Chapter 4.

Table 16 may be compared with Table 17, which shows the age profile of all academic staff in the public universities in 1998/9.

[11] Some critical schools and departments, such as the Medical School, use a substantially larger percentage of contract staff.

The two tables show a negligible percentage of staff under the age of 30 in both 1998/9 and 2002. While the age cohorts are more spread out in Table 17 than in Table 16, the 41–50 group forms the bulk of staff in all the universities, with more than 50 per cent of the UEW staff in that age group. Staff over 50 are also numerous, accounting for nearly 40 per cent at the University of Ghana. Overall, the staff of Ghanaian universities are ageing, and few young faculty members are joining the pool. Even in the younger universities (UDS and UEW), the staff are not young. Then again the UDS, with fewer staff, has more than 40 per cent under the age of 40. The ageing faculty reflects the slow pace of postgraduate training and the slow absorption of students into academia, which has implications for the maintenance of quality, given the growth in student numbers reported in Chapter 4.

Figure 5 gives an indication of the factors that faculty members considered important in terms of motivation to stay in their posts. Five factors were rated almost equally: remuneration; learning facilities; teaching and research facilities; research funding and the working environment.

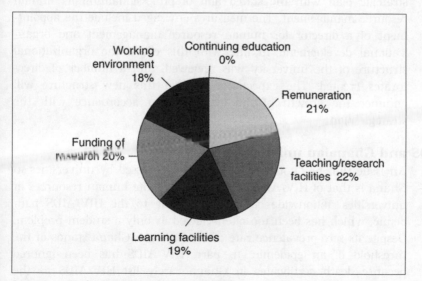

Source: From Faculty Survey, Ghana Case Study, 2002.

Figure 5: Motivation of faculty members

Figure 5 reveals that satisfactory remuneration levels alone might not be enough for universities to attract and retain staff. Efforts are needed to improve their work environment and facilities. The extent to which staff can operate effectively and efficiently is greatly influenced by the structures within which they operate, and appropriate mechanisms need to be developed and maintained for this purpose.

In addition to academic staff, well-trained senior administrative staff are needed to establish and maintain quality assurance systems at all levels. In discussions with members of the Ghana Association of University Administrators (GAUA), concerns were raised about their limited opportunities for professional development compared with those of teaching staff. As student numbers expand, the pool of senior administrative and technical staff should also keep pace.

Recruitment and retention of teaching and research staff are critical and should be done in the context of its human resource policies. Measures to attract and retain high quality staff at all professional and administrative levels should therefore be introduced.

The University of Ghana addressed this concern in its second strategic plan with the stated aim of professionalizing its human resource management. The measures envisaged include the appointment of a director for human resource management and organizational development. In line with this effort, the organizational structure of the university was reviewed, and a number of directorates created. The expectation is that this new structure will enhance the growth of the institution in accordance with the strategic plan.

HIV/AIDS and Ghanaian universities

An issue that has not been adequately addressed by universities in Ghana is that of HIV/AIDS. Yet the inadequate human resources at universities nationwide could worsen due to the HIV/AIDS pandemic, which has been too often viewed as only a student problem. Despite its sero-prevalence rate of 3.4 per cent, Ghana stands at the threshold of an epidemic. In part, HIV/AIDS has been ignored because death certificates in Ghana rarely list HIV/AIDS as the cause, which has allowed too many people to pretend that all is well.

In our discussions with university administrators, faculty, workers

94

and students, the issue of HIV/AIDS was not raised. When prompted, responses focused on students who were perceived to be most at risk and in need of education. Respondents cited the lectures on AIDS in the universities' freshman orientation programmes as evidence of engagement with the pandemic. These lectures mostly promote safe sexual health through abstinence or the use of condoms. Student representative councils and medical students also organize AIDS' awareness weeks. While HIV/AIDS is addressed as a component in courses on population and health, there are no general courses on the subject, beyond a few early efforts undertaken at the urging of agencies such as the United Nations Fund for Population Activities (UNFPA). At the University of Cape Coast, the Centre for Development Studies made reference to a research study on the effects of HIV/AIDS on students at the various campuses.

Workers' groups such as FUSSAG and TEWU also stated that they had attended workshops on HIV/AIDS. Discussions with members of TEWU/FUSSAG at the University of Ghana revealed that three TEWU members had died from HIV/AIDS in 2001, and union executives considered this sufficiently important to put forward some remedial initiatives, mainly in the area of education.

At KNUST, following the attendance of the Vice-Chancellor at an AAU conference in Nairobi in 2001 where Dr Michael Kelly presented a report on HIV/AIDS at African universities, a committee was set up to work on the problem. However, the focus was once again on students (Focus group discussion with University Teachers Association of Ghana Executive, KNUST, February 2002).

Particularly at the University of Ghana – where the Noguchi Memorial Institute has been at the forefront of research into HIV/AIDS and was among the first to test for the disease in Ghana – the lack of an integrated approach attending to all sectors of the university population is inexcusable. The denial and inaction are of particular concern at universities where high levels of transactional sex occur and many allegations of sexual harassment among students, staff and workers are reported, as discussed in Chapter 9.

In general, the universities have not given adequate thought or attention to HIV/AIDS as a problem in the university community or to their potential leadership role as experts in knowledge production. Nor have they contemplated the potential impact of loss of staff through illness or death on teaching, administration and other

95

university functions. The universities need to take the challenge of HIV/AIDS seriously and to integrate it more fully into their teaching and research activities.

Financial resource mobilization & management

University financing is a major issue in Ghana. As public institutions, universities are financed primarily by the government and through their own revenue-generating activities, fees paid by students, private donations and external agencies. The major stakeholders share three concerns about funding: (i) the adequacy and timeliness of funding; (ii) the sharing of responsibilities for funding; and (iii) the utilization and management of resources.

In Ghana, the public universities rely mainly on the government for resources. For a long time, they were funded through line-item budgeting which listed emoluments, other recurrent expenditures, including capital expenditure and investment. As part of the educational reforms described in Chapter 3, a programme-linked budgeting system was introduced based on full-time equivalent student numbers as a basis for allocating financial resources to universities for their recurrent expenditures. However, this approach did not take sufficient account of capital and investment expenditures or historical factors. The current system uses the Medium Term Expenditure Framework (MTEF), which treats the annual budget within a three-year framework.

Table 18: Funding levels for universities: 1991/92–2000/01 (in Ghana cedi

	1991/2	92/93	93/94	94/95
Enrolment	11,857	14,278	15,183	18,000
Funding (¢ bn)	12,235	12,451	16,986	23,567
Cedi funding per student (¢ m.)	1.03188	0.87204	1.11875	1.30928
Average exchange rate ¢/$	437.09	716.67	964.55	1,210.76
Dollar cost per student	2,360.74	1,216.79	1.159.86	1.081.37
Direct teaching costs, (45%) of total	1062.3	547.55	521.94	486.82

a) refers to estimates.
Sources: Addae-Mensah, 2001:47; NCTE, 2002.

Trends and tribulations in public funding

Between 1990 and 2000, recurrent expenditures for education were estimated at between 3 and 5 per cent of GDP (Addae-Mensah, 2000). According to Addae-Mensah (2001), the average annual dollar value of the government subvention per student paid to the universities dwindled from $2,360 in 1991 to $566 in 2000, a decline of nearly 75 per cent in one decade, as shown in Table 18.

Even though the funding per student increased fourfold in cedi terms, its real value fell, due to inflation and the dependence on imports for many of the institutional needs such as laboratory equipment, books, journals and other consumables. In addition to these material resources, human resources have foreign-exchange components in their recruitment and training, which is the reason for converting cedis to dollars in this analysis. However, local inflation differs from its depreciation in dollar terms; these data must therefore be interpreted with caution.

The precarious situation of government funding led the major stakeholders to adopt the 'Akosombo Accord' in 1997, a cost-sharing arrangement under which 70 per cent of funding comes from the government with the remaining 30 per cent distributed equally between three sources: internal revenue-generation, private donations and student tuition payments (PEF, 1997). The implementation of this accord has been fraught with major difficulties.

Until the 1990s, universities had no incentive to generate funds. On the contrary, they were actively discouraged from doing so, in

96/97[a]	97/98[a]	98/99[a]	99/00[a]	00/01[a]
23,126	26,684	31,501	36,221	40,673
53,346	56,842	76,734	108,671	162,935
2.30675	2.13019	2.43592	3.00022	4.000597
2,070.49	2,318.96	2,930.45	5,237.3	7,0769.5
1.114.1	918.6	831.2	572.9	566.1 Direct
501.34	413.37	374.04	257.8	254.75

97

keeping with a public sector ethos and through reciprocal funding cuts when other resources were raised. To encourage institutions to generate more of their own funding now, the NCTE has assured universities that it will no longer reduce its support in response to internally generated funds. Other internal funding incentives have also been proposed.

Worldwide, universities generate income through student fees. But in Ghana institutions are not permitted to charge Ghanaian students tuition fees, in line with social democratic principles established by the first post-independence government. In 2001, there were major public debates when the Vice-Chancellor of the University of Ghana announced new tuition fees for students who could afford to pay. The university viewed this as a means both of increasing enrolment and of mobilizing necessary financial resources to aid in its operations. The ensuing debate pitted the university authorities against a militant student leadership, buttressed in part by the government's commitment to provide 70 per cent of the cost of university education.

Interestingly, over 70 per cent of respondents in our student survey indicated that they were prepared to pay more for quality education. However, when asked to suggest where funding increases might come from, most respondents identified public sources: Government of Ghana scholarships (33 per cent); District Assemblies, which also draw their funding from the Consolidated Fund (18 per cent); support from the private sector (24 per cent), with the remainder from family sources and own income (15 per cent). This information is shown in Table 19.

Table 19: Recommended sources for funding increases

Funding Source	% recommended
Family source	7.5
Own income	7.3
District Assembly	18.0
Ghana Government scholarship	33.0
Support from private sector enterprises	24.6
Employer	7.7
Other	1.8
Total	100.0

Source: Survey of University Students conducted as part of the Ghana Universities Case Study, 2002.

The decline of public educational funding is affected further by the government's system of financial allocation, which has undergone several changes from its original quinquennial allocations through line-item budgeting and then programme-linked budgeting to the current Medium Term Expenditure Framework (MTEF). The MTEF system, started in 1998, requires a three-year expenditure framework, but it does not directly address the fundamental issues of inadequate funding and delays in the release of funds.

It is helpful to understand the operation of the MTEF. The NCTE views student numbers as the primary basis for the funding of universities, which suggests that the training of students is seen as their only activity. In challenging the universities' cost calculations, students refer to the cost of 'what is required to train them'. However, the full cost of university education includes far more than the training of students, and encompasses activities such as research, community service, policy engagement, and outreach, all of which may not be covered if student numbers serve as the primary basis for resource disbursement.

A further source of decline in funding endowments arises from the budget allocation process. Initial allocations are directed to the tertiary education sector as a whole, after which the NCTE advises on their distribution among institutions in the sector, including universities. As part of the Poverty Reduction Strategy, the Ministry of Education is allocating 12 per cent of the education budget to tertiary education, down from the current 15 per cent (Republic of Ghana, 2003a).

Once these funds are released, there are similar developments at the university level. According to NCTE norms, subvention funds should be disbursed in the following proportions: direct academic costs, 45 per cent; general education expenses, 15 per cent; library costs, 10 per cent; central administration expenses, 6 per cent; student facilities, 5 per cent; municipal services, 15 per cent; and miscellaneous expenses, 4 per cent (NCTE, 1999). Although direct academic costs are supposed to cover teaching, the government subvention barely covers the salaries budget. For example, at the University of Ghana, the government subvention in 2002 was 72.7 billion cedis, out of which 55 billion (76 per cent) went in emoluments. In that same year, the research and awards fund was 13.8 billion, of which 8.1 billion cedis (58 per cent) came from central government sources (UG, 2002b).

99

Since student numbers have become the most important factor in determining subventions, an unwitting drive to increase student numbers has confounded the desire to limit student admissions and programmes to what can reasonably be covered by the available resources. Consequently, while NCTE norms call for restructuring the growth in annual admissions to no more than 10 per cent, the actual increase at the University of Ghana has been around 14 per cent (UG, 2002a).

University-generated revenue

Beyond government subventions and the Academic Facilities User Fee (AFUF), some departments have developed diversified sources of funding, such as projects and other linkage activities. The total percentage of revenue generated internally in these universities increased from 7.7 per cent in 1996 to 26 per cent in 2000 (Adu and Opoku-Afriyie, 2002). In 2002, the University of Ghana, for example, generated as much as 38 per cent of its income through internally generated funds: government subventions totalled nearly 73 billion cedis, while about 45 billion cedis came from internally generated funds, notably student fees (UG, 2002a). These internal funding sources should be managed, however, without diverting energies away from the universities' core activities.

Most of the public universities have sought private investment in areas like student accommodation, while using government funds (including the GetFund) to provide and improve infrastructure, such as lecture rooms and other services. University finance committees, reporting to the University Council, guide these spending deliberations. The Development Committee, on the other hand, is responsible for physical development, and these two committees must work closely together.

In discussions with the various groups, neither students nor the university authorities raised the issue of public funding for university education. Instead, the focus was on the way the universities deal with limited resources. In our opinion, this silence has created missed opportunities for co-operation between students and university leaders in the elaboration of educational policies.

External funding

External funding is important to universities in Ghana. Activities normally covered by this include government grants and loans for

100

educational development, specific project grants, collaborative arrangements with other entities and funding for visiting scholars such as Fulbright grants.

While aggregated figures for external funding at each institution are difficult to obtain, anecdotal evidence suggests that these resources have dwindled during the last three decades, with some traditional donors ceasing direct support to universities in favour of basic education. Table 20 shows donor contributions as a proportion of annual estimates for the education sector as a whole.

Table 20: Major sources of funding within the education sector, 1999–2001, cedis bn

Source	1999	2000	2001
Government of Ghana	678,549	972,682	1,299,754
Donor	90,340	60,264	120,460
Total	768,889	1,032,946	1,422,360

Source: Ghana Education Service, Administration and Finance Division, 2002, cited in Republic of Ghana, 2002a.

It is not clear that this table includes all external resources received by the universities in the years in question. The levels and range of sources of funding vary among universities. For the University of Ghana, DANIDA has been a major source of funding for the past decade, contributing to: a remote sensing facility at the Department of Geography and Resource Development; funds for ICT development and for an intra-universities library connectivity project; a market for the use of staff and students; and a new building for the Institute of African Studies.

According to the counterpart team from the University of Ghana, some externally funded programmes under way at the university in 2001/2 were:

- the Centre for African Wetlands, a regional centre focusing on conservation and wetlands, currently funded by the Dutch government with US$950,000;
- the Volta Basin Research Project, a US$750,000 four-year study funded by the Volta River Authority, which aims to mitigate the impact of dams on the people of the Lower Volta Basin;

101

- a consortium of four African universities and the London School of Hygiene and Tropical Medicine, funded by a US$40,000,000 grant from the Bill and Melinda Gates Foundation, to establish centres for the treatment and control of malaria;
- the Ford Foundation $800,000 grant to the Institute of African Studies for research on chieftaincy;
- the African Regional Postgraduate Programme in Insect Science (ARPPIS), funded with about $250,000 by the German Academic Exchange Programme (DAAD);
- the Multi-Centre Growth Reference Study, given about $450,000 by the World Health Organization;
- the United Nations University project on People, Land and Environment ($318,640);
- the Norwegian Universities Funded Research (NUFU) project on Computational Lexicography and Language Development ($523,385);
- an NUFU research project on Tradition and Modernity in Ghanaian History and Development ($616,591);
- the USAID-funded Bean-cowpea Collaborative Research Support Program ($450,000).

Through link agreements with several American and European universities as well as external funding agencies, KNUST has also received support from DANIDA, the UK Department for International Development (DFID) and the Canadian International Development Agency (CIDA), among others, for various programmes around the university. Similarly, the University of Cape Coast also had a number of externally funded programmes and projects, while the UEW and UDS had fewer such programmes and projects because of their relative size and status as newer institutions.

The GETFund

Over the years, government subventions have been barely adequate for emoluments. Currently, both students and faculty feel that teaching, learning and research facilities need more support. Growing student numbers and technical changes call for more classroom, laboratory and office space. Where facilities are available, the appropriate equipment and consumables are either unavailable or insufficient. In the past, the Public Investment Programme (PIP) provided for adequate capital and development expenditures, but this has been replaced by the recently established GetFund.

The GETFund, set up in 2001 by an Act of Parliament (Act 581), has positively influenced the funding of tertiary education in Ghana. The object of the fund is to finance all levels of education by the government. The funds are to be expended as follows:

- to provide financial support through the Ministry of Education for essential academic facilities and infrastructure in public educational institutions;
- to provide supplementary funding to the Scholarships Secretariat for gifted but needy students;
- to contribute monies to student loans in accredited tertiary institutions;
- to provide, through the National Council on Tertiary Education, grants to train the best students for research and teaching programmes;
- to provide support to and promote other educational programmes as needed.

Monies for GETFund come from a 2.5 per cent increase in the Value Added Tax, specifically intended to support education. A fund administrator and a board oversee its work, and all allocations under the fund are subject to Parliamentary approval. Out of the total of 140 billion cedis disbursed in 2001, 125 billion went to tertiary institutions, including support for student loans. The amounts approved for all tertiary institutions were 60 billion cedis in 2001 and 149 billion cedis in 2002; universities received 66 and 56 per cent thereof respectively. However, from figures available at the GETFund website (www.getfund.org), actual amounts disbursed differed from amounts initially approved. Apart from two institutions which were able to spend the whole of their approved amounts and another that overspent by 40 per cent, most of the institutions used from 17 to 89 per cent of their total approved funding.

The fund has recently come under scrutiny for several reasons. The Minister of Finance, in his 2003 national budget statement, noted that the government was in arrears in its payment in support of the GETFund and was seeking Parliamentary approval to make up this shortage over five years. Subsequent to this statement, the

103

National Union of Ghana Students (NUGS) threatened to sue the government for defaulting in its payments as stipulated under the GETFund Act. The NUGS and the government have also disagreed about the actual amounts owed to the fund. In addition, some members of the public have expressed concern that the government is using the fund as a substitute for, rather than a supplement to, government subventions to the tertiary educational sector.

Students have argued that since university education benefits everyone, students unable to pay should not have to do so. They cite Article 15 of the Constitution, which states that 'higher education shall be made equally accessible to all on the basis of capacity by every appropriate means, and in particular, by the progressive intro-duction of free education'.

A number of institutions have also criticized the cumbersome procedures for utilizing allocated funds. Some would prefer to have more responsibility over these funding arrangements, and fewer restrictions, such as having to acquire contracts before the release of funds to suppliers.

The criteria used by the fund administrators in the selection of proposed projects are also unclear. For example, the universities' requests totalled 913 billion cedis for 2003, nearly seven times larger than the amount approved in 2002. The actual amounts allocated were much smaller, so institutions have to reprioritize their projects. Alternatively, the fund and the institutions could make five-year projections, so that funding could become more predictable and coherent over time. Furthermore, the institutions have not been required to relate these capital budgets to their strategic and master plans. Such correlations would help rationalize these educational expenditures at both the university and national levels.

Indications for the future

While the government tries to increase support for university education, there are other competing claims on these public funds. For example, even within the tertiary sector, while funding per university student fell from about $1,100 in 1996/97 to about $580 in 2000/2001, equivalent figures for polytechnics were $323 and $212 respectively. These discrepancies in funding levels across sectors in education are unlikely to change.

In addition to government funding, traditional authorities, District

Assemblies and private bodies seem willing to support tertiary education with scholarships, need-based support and other gifts and donations. These sources could make a difference in university funding, but they are unlikely to be sustained or adequate, even when combined with other external sources.

As noted earlier, internally generated income has increased, mostly from student tuition fees. However, this means that a small number of students pay more than most of their peers. The challenge is to find ways to generate enough funds from these sources, since other resources are insufficient.

In addition to human and financial resources, ICT cuts across all university operations and could dramatically change the modes of operation and management of resources, if properly harnessed. The next chapter addresses this subject.

7 The Use of Information & Communication Technologies in Teaching, Learning & Management Services

Information and communication technologies (ICTs) have undergone dramatic changes in the last twenty years and continue to change at an amazing rate. ICT resources are expensive to purchase and maintain. Many developing countries, particularly in sub-Saharan Africa, find it difficult to keep up with technological change, leading to the 'digital divide' between the developed and developing worlds. However, as information and knowledge become more critical for economic and social development, developing countries have no choice but to exploit ICTs to the fullest extent possible. This chapter reviews attempts by universities to incorporate ICTs into their core activities.

ICTs here refer to all information receiving, processing, storing and communication technologies. In the past, these technologies were separate and independent, but current developments are bringing them together, in turn affecting and, in some instances, determining the way institutions operate. This process of convergence has had a major effect on university operations.

Three broad areas of ICT usage are reviewed in this chapter: academic (teaching, learning, research and extension); administration and management (student records, the management of human resources, financial records, physical assets and information and communications); and libraries (access to information). Factors considered are: university ICT policy and its relation to national ICT policy; structures of ICT facilities; examples of value–added activities such as software development; and the use of ICT facilities to achieve institutional goals.

The ICT environment in Ghana

Computers have been used in Ghana since the 1960s. In some universities, they have been employed for processing payrolls, student admissions and examinations as well as for teaching and learning in a few academic departments. The use of computers spread dramatically with the advent of the Internet, starting in 1989/90 with a pilot project by the Pan African Development Information System

(PADIS) and the International Development Research Centre (IDRC) to bring dial-up electronic communication to the Ghana National Scientific and Technological Information Network (GHASTINET), the AAU and the Technology Transfer Centre (TTC). Full commercial Internet connectivity was available by 1995, as a result of the pioneering work of Network Computer Systems (NCS). University libraries took the lead in bringing these facilities to their institutions, and the University of Ghana library is still active in providing Internet services and ICT training. Since 1995, the number of Internet Service Providers (ISPs) has also expanded dramatically.

With the increase in the number of phone lines available in Ghana, cybercafés have proliferated, especially in large cities, along with commercial fax, telephone and copy communication centres. Telephone density has increased from 0.3 to 1.3 lines per 1,000 persons. The number of mobile phones has also increased dramatically, with four authorized service providers. The government also hopes to extend telephone service to every town where there is a school or training college.

The private sector has led the public sector, including government and universities, in its usage of ICT resources, its ability to recruit and retain IT professionals and its institutional impact.

ICT policies

Ghana promulgated an ICT policy in 2003 – *the Ghana ICT for Accelerated Development (ICT4AD) Policy* (Republic of Ghana, 2003b), with the following vision statement:

To improve the quality of life of the people of Ghana by significantly enriching their social, economic and cultural well-being through the rapid development and modernization of the economy and society using information and communication technologies as the main engine for accelerated and sustainable economic and social development.

Three broad policy goals are identified therein:

• developing Ghana's information society and economy;
• pursuing multi-sectoral ICT-led socio-economic development goals; and
• expanding Ghana's ICT sector and using it as a broad-based enabler of development goals.

107

The document outlines the following objectives specifically for education:

- to facilitate the deployment, utilization and exploitation of ICT within the educational system to improve educational access and delivery and to support teaching and learning from primary school upwards;
- to modernize the educational system to improve the quality of education and training at all levels of the system and to expand access to education, training and research resources and facilities;
- to orientate all levels of the country's educational system to the teaching and learning of science and technology in order to accelerate the spread of science and technology in society and to produce a critical mass of requisite human resources and a well-informed citizenry;
- to achieve universal basic education and improve the level of basic and computer literacy in the country;
- to ensure that all citizens are at least functionally literate and productive;
- to expand and increase access to secondary and tertiary education;
- to strengthen science education at all levels and in all aspects of the educational system, especially at the basic and secondary school levels.

The policy document further addresses the implementation of these objectives. No university strategic plan has yet incorporated any reference to the national ICT policy, which was only recently adopted. In interviews, two institutions reported that they had an institutional ICT policy (UG and KNUST) – although few respondents were aware of it – while the UCC and UEW had no ICT policy at the time of the survey. However, the four institutions surveyed (UG, KNUST, UCC and UEW) have made commitments to the development of ICT at their institutions. For example, in the University of Ghana's strategic plan, one of the 'key strategic thrusts' is to:

design and operate a reliable, functional, relevant and cost-effective Information and Communication Technology (ICT) system and related services to drive all initiatives (UG, 2001).

108

Similarly, an objective of the KNUST strategic plan is to: 'Make computer literacy an essential part of the training at the university and promote the use of information technology to increase productivity and efficiency' (KNUST, 2001). The UEW has planned new programmes to train teachers to teach ICT in secondary schools. It also reveals a commitment to using ICT to improve teaching methods. The UCC refers to the objective of providing 'integrated modern ICT facilities' in its strategic plan (UCC, 2000). None of the documents, however, demonstrates how the institutions expect their ICT activities and policies to impact on the nation as a whole, since the emphasis is mainly on improved institutional productivity.

ICT structures & systems

There are four broad areas of ICT application in the universities, namely: academic, administrative, library and general. The structures in each of these areas are discussed in detail below.

Academic needs

Although only the University of Ghana and KNUST have computer science departments that offer undergraduate degree programmes, all the universities have ICT programmes. ICT facilities are used to enhance the teaching and learning process in virtually every department. The University of Ghana has received a grant from the Carnegie Corporation to establish a computer-assisted teaching and learning resource centre, expand its ICT infrastructure and strengthen the use of ICT facilities in the library as well as management and administration.

At the time of the study, the Computer Science Department at the University of Ghana had 35 computers for 400 students, while KNUST's Computer Science Department had 100 computers for 500 students. Universities have had difficulty in attracting ICT staff, as evidenced by the severe understaffing and high staff turnover rates of the Computer Science departments at UG and KNUST.

The ICT study commissioned as part of the case study explored ICT use by academic staff and students. ICT facilities received the lowest ratings on user satisfaction and availability from both groups, in comparison with other university facilities. The results of this survey are shown in Tables 21 and 22.

109

Table 21: Faculty satisfaction with access to facilities (%)

Facilities	Low	Average	High
Library	45.6	42.3	12.1
ICT facilities	71.1	23.8	5.1
Other teaching & research facilities	59.1	37.3	3.6

Source: Budu et al., 2002.

Table 22: Students' satisfaction with facilities (%)

Facilities	Low	Average	High
Classroom space	59.2	31.8	8.6
Teaching facilities	49.2	45.2	5.3
Learning facilities	50.4	44.1	5.3
Library facilities	33.1	54.8	11.9
ICT facilities	76.4	18.9	3.3
Bookshop	46.1	42.5	8.4
Laboratories	54.4	31.9	4.7

Source: ibid.

Table 23 reveals that as many as 44 per cent of the students surveyed had very low expectations of acquiring ICT skills as opposed to skills in other areas during their programmes of study.

All the universities surveyed have made efforts to improve ICT availability by setting up computer pools, intranet and Internet facilities along with structures to promote the use of these facilities in teaching and learning. Some campuses have a computer-aided distance-education unit, supported through the African Virtual

Table 23: Students' expectation of skills to be acquired (%)

Skills	Low	Average	High
Interpersonal skills	4.1	34.2	61.8
IT skills	44.1	40.5	15.4
Professional skills	6.4	29.8	63.7
Skills to live comfortably	5.6	45.8	48.6
Adaptability to job demands	6.4	33.8	59.8

Source: ibid.

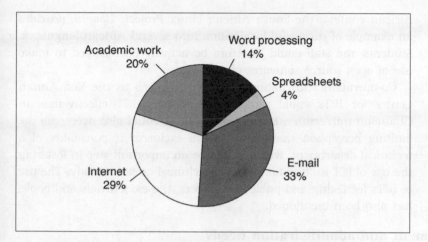

Figure 6: Use of information technology facilities

University. Students use ICT facilities for e-mail and to search the web as well as for academic work (see Figure 6), but more resources and training are needed to broaden access and expose students to the full potential of ICTs.

As noted above, the new national ICT policy aims to use ICT to accelerate economic growth and development. To facilitate this, university graduates will need to be competent in ICT use, and academic staff will need the skills to fully use the medium and train students in its use. The University of Cape Coast and the University of Education, Winneba teacher training programmes could prove beneficial to this effort. In an initiative that must be encouraged, some departments have contracted with the private sector to set up computer facilities and to train students.

At the moment, there is no single institutional structure to support ICT learning, and departments are free to adapt and use such facilities as they deem fit. While some progress has been achieved, departments need to acquire appropriate software, such as SPSS and AutoCAD, to facilitate learning. In addition, open source software is increasingly becoming an alternative to proprietary software, and developing countries such as India, Brazil and South Africa are integrating it into their tertiary education system. Besides being free, the possibility of localizing open source software is one of the main largely untapped potentials it holds especially in the

111

African context; the South African Linux Project, *Ubuntu*, provides an example of successful localization into several African languages. Students and staff could therefore be actively encouraged to make use of open source software solutions.

Co-operation with national ICT centres such as the Kofi Annan Centre for ICTs could significantly enhance ICT effectiveness in Ghanaian universities. Mainstreaming ICTs could also overcome the limiting perception that they are the exclusive responsibility of a technical department, which would be an important step in fostering the use of ICT in 'traditionally non-technical' areas of study. The use of ICTs for listing and publishing papers, theses, journals and books has also been mentioned.

Management and administration needs

ICT facilities for administration are also important to educational institutions for the realization of their institutional goals. Structures in place vary widely due to historical factors. At KNUST, UCC and UEW, the planning units oversee management computing, while at the University of Ghana, this responsibility falls on the Data Processing Centre (DPC), which was established in 1987 to perform three main functions:

- development and implementation of computerized information systems;
- training of staff in ICT facilities and use; and
- provision of ICT services to the university community.

However, the main focus has been on the first function due to a number of factors, including staff and other resource constraints. The planning units in the other three universities were established during the early 1990s, as part of the education reform exercise, to design and implement institutional information management systems. In addition to these centrally located units, the finance sections at the three universities have their own IT professionals. However, staff turnover in these sections is high, due to unattractive conditions of work.

In general, the public universities have a relatively long history of ICT use for management. The early payroll, admission and examination systems, which were locally developed and maintained using

112

stand-alone software, have now become obsolete. However, Ghanaian universities have made a little progress towards the globally accepted standard of integrated software for management and administration. With World Bank funding in 1997, the Ministry of Education acquired the Integrated Tertiary System (ITS), an integrated software package, for the UG, UCC and KNUST. The software was designed to handle student records, human resource management, finance, and physical facilities management. Its implementation has not been as successful as it could have been, due to several factors:

- limited hardware availability
- absence of reliable infrastructure
- insufficient management commitment to systems integration
- high rates of ICT staff turnover
- lack of funds to cover maintenance, training and systems development
- lack of appreciation of the complexities of implementation
- inadequate ICT professional staff
- inadequate adaptation of the software to the Ghanaian context and to the user needs of Ghanaian staff.

The universities have been most successful in computerizing and integrating their student records. Of the three campuses where the ITS was introduced, the University of Ghana has made the most progress. Its student records system is in place, with work proceeding to add more functions to it, and it is working on the human resources management module, assisted by a recent grant from the Carnegie Corporation. The UCC and KNUST have not implemented ITS for their human resources and finance systems, continuing to handle the records either on locally developed stand-alone systems or manually.

While the universities are in the process of setting up campus-wide area networks connected to the Internet and to local area networks, paper communication is still dominant. There are also no institutional structures for conducting business over the telephone and by electronic means. The UEW and the UDS face the greatest challenge here, because their campuses are spread over long distances with few telephone lines and unreliable power supply (see Figure 4 showing the location of the universities).

113

The use of ICT in libraries

Libraries on university campuses have been major contributors to the provision of ICT services. A summary of the ICT usage at the universities follows, based on Kisiedu (2002).

University of Ghana

The University of Ghana's central library, the Balme Library, is the most technologically advanced university library in Ghana. It has its own electronic support unit and maintains an electronic catalogue that is accessible to all campus-networked computers. Apart from the Balme Library, there are other specialized libraries based in faculties, institutes and schools and the College of Health Sciences, with varying degrees of automation and ICT facilities.

The telecommunication system of the University of Ghana has recently been upgraded with the assistance of DANIDA. The university is residential, and employees' houses have direct access telephone lines (for those who want and can afford them). The campus intercom system has also been improved and expanded to all departments.

KNUST

The KNUST library has greatly benefited from an expanded infrastructure of electronic equipment, especially through the ITS project which brought many computers to the library. The library has full Internet connectivity through a VSAT,[12] and is a node of the Consortium of Academic and Research Libraries in Ghana (CARLIGH).[13] Library users can also search a number of subscription online catalogues and obtain copies of documents. The library's stock of microcomputers has grown from one or two in 1996 to 60 at present. Fifty-five machines are in use for Internet searches and five in the work areas.

Generally, the telecommunication infrastructure is satisfactory, at least by local standards. KNUST has just completed installation of a fibre optic backbone network for the campus with the help of Ghana Telecom, which will expand Internet access to all faculties and

---

[12] VSAT (*very small aperture terminal*) is an earthbound station for satellite communications.

[13] CARLIGH was adopted as the name of the former Ghana Interlibrary Lending and Document Delivery Network GILLDDNET in 2003.

departments. It has also recently acquired a technician to handle basic electronic support.

The University for Development Studies

ICT infrastructure development at the UDS has been gradual but systematic, although totally donor-based. The university recently acquired a VSAT for Internet access, and the telecommunication infrastructure has also been improved.

The University of Cape Coast

The UCC has full Internet connectivity through its own VSAT, and the campus has improved its electronic capacity with a fibre optic backbone. The library has CD-ROM facilities, the Bibliophile citations tool and CDS-ISIS software for cataloguing, as well as a staff member trained in basic computer maintenance.

Co-operation and networking among Ghana's public university libraries

The Committee of University Librarians and their Deputies (CULD) has promoted networking and co-operation among member libraries, with recent efforts directed at building a consortium of university libraries in Ghana. The Open Society Institute (OSI) also held a meeting in Accra in 2004 that defined a framework for a consortium of Ghanaian university and research libraries. These initiatives give some cause for optimism.

General facilities

Private providers of ICT facilities are present on all the university campuses, and in most instances operate independently of the official university facilities, with a resulting duplication of effort and high cost. Some collaboration could be worked out to the benefit of all.

There are not many examples of inter-university collaboration in the use and management of ICT facilities, and the few joint efforts have either failed or moved slowly. Co-operation in this area would be highly desirable to eliminate unnecessary duplication of scarce and expensive facilities. Internet provision to universities is a case in point. A DANIDA-funded project supplied a VSAT to the University of Ghana, which was intended to serve the UCC and KNUST as well.

115

However, the connections to the other universities developed a number of problems, and the two institutions proceeded to acquire their own VSATs.

Another ICT area in need of attention is that of the development of local content. Many university users are accessing materials on the Internet that are not appropriate to the Ghanaian context. More emphasis needs to be placed on Internet dissemination of local research and resources.

Suggestions for the future

ICT facilities are subject to the same concerns raised in relation to other resources in Chapter 6 on resource mobilization and management. However, they also present specific concerns, which are briefly discussed below.

Human resource development: This is an area that needs major emphasis and creative thinking at the university level to supply the trained personnel that the country needs to implement the national ICT policy.

Development and management of ICT facilities: Universities should familiarize themselves with the national ICT policy (Republic of Ghana, 2003b), to ensure that their plans fit with the national vision for ICT development.

Spreading the cost of ICT: Because of the high cost of ICT facilities, avenues for collaboration and economies of scale should be explored by each institution at sectoral and institutional levels, as well as with the private sector.

Summary

This chapter has shown that the development and use of ICT facilities is critical to the economic development of Ghana. Compared with the private sector, universities lag behind in ICTs. The use of ICTs yields information-processing and storage advantages of vital importance in the 'knowledge industry'. In many instances, even small investments in hardware are not supported by software and

116

human capital. The result is often the under-utilization of resources.

University leadership is also needed in ICT development. Persistent efforts by institutions will have a significant impact. Given the resource-intensive nature of ICT facilities, this is a fertile area for collaboration among institutions, despite the earlier setbacks that have occurred.

8 Governance & Participation

Democratization processes in/outside universities

In this study, we defined governance as collective deliberation and decision-making, and the development of stakeholder relations to improve the mobilization, allocation and management of university resources. Three dimensions of governance were examined: first, the representativeness of university governance institutions and their responsiveness to stakeholders; second, the mode of governance, including the efficiency, effectiveness and accountability of management processes; and third, issues of leadership, especially strategic leadership, in the direction of change.

University institutions are not isolated from national developments, as illustrated in Chapter 3. In the prevailing democratic conditions and trying economic times, universities can influence efforts to consolidate democracy and manage the economy more effectively, as discussed in Chapter 1.

Autonomy & governance

As noted in Chapter 3, universities in Ghana have become largely autonomous in their governance. At present, all five publicly funded universities appoint their own Chancellors and constitute their Councils, in consultation with the government. Government nominees vary in number on university councils, but the government appoints the chairs. The composition of councils reflects the full range of interests in universities, including workers' representatives, academic staff and students. In addition, the government often nominates eminent persons from industry, ICT, the judiciary or faith-based groups.

The most far-reaching governance process is in the appointment of Vice-Chancellors, which is based on elaborate recruitment procedures managed entirely by the universities. Recent appointments of new Vice-Chancellors in all five publicly funded universities showed high levels of competition and transparency, with considerable public interest in the process. In all five universities, pro-Vice Chancellors (pro-VCs) are elected from among their peers to assist and support the Vice-Chancellors; the first pro-VC was elected at the UDS in 2002. At present, each of these universities has only one pro-VC, although the University of Ghana's strategic plan proposes the appointment of at least two more pro-VCs – one for academic affairs and the other for operations, planning and diversity. A myriad of committees on academic and non-academic matters and staff is involved in decision-making in all universities.

Governance, participation & accountability

University decision-making is generally regarded as slow, due to a strong emphasis on consultation and consensus-building among competing interests. Committee meetings are often long in duration and short on results. This has prompted a number of universities to decentralize their decision-making procedures to accelerate the process. At the UCC, for example, many decisions, including resource allocations, are now made at the departmental level, reducing transaction costs and the time for implementation with respect to departmental needs. Stakeholder involvement at this level has also been enhanced, through consultations with staff and students. The UCC's achievements notwithstanding, decentralization has been criticized for exacerbating departmental individualism and the balkanization of university services. The result has been the costly duplication of services at the departmental level and a growing resistance to co-operation and resource-sharing within the university community.

In our visits to universities, we were struck by the divergence of views among deans, directors and other university administrators and faculty, in contrast to the consistent defence of the university as one system through the Teachers' and Educational Workers' Union (TEWU). Indeed, the TEWU is the only campus association that is a member of the Trades Union Congress (TUC) of Ghana. While all junior staff of the university belong to the TEWU, senior staff can also join it, which links TEWU and FUSSAG. The TEWU is also represented on university Councils, and its members are known for their militancy and willingness to strike.

TEWU members often have access to opportunities for study within their universities, and several of their leaders now have university degrees. Many of these leaders have remained TEWU

119

members, bringing a higher level of knowledge and some sophistication to the union and its activities. Their university positions have exposed them firsthand to its workings, and they reflect this knowledge in their aspirations for the university. Of all the groups we met, they were the ones who openly championed the need for change, raising issues about institutional cultures, the use of resources, the legality of certain administrative actions and the need for the university to represent all of its constituencies.

At the core of the reforms in university governance are the systems of financial management and accountability. In at least three of the five universities studied, on-going revisions of financial systems were improving financial control and accountability. But this process has been far less transparent than these systems suggest. Workers and students in the three universities (UCC, KNUST, UG) have questioned the new methods of budgeting and resource allocation. In particular, university investment decisions, the balancing of senior members' benefits vis-à-vis university needs, and the arithmetic of financial expenses and fee calculations are areas of real concern.

Strategic leadership

As noted earlier, the onerous challenges of coping with crises have forestalled the emergence of long-term strategic visions of transformation, thereby constraining university leadership. Co-operation among stakeholders – workers, students, academic and administrative staff – has been rare in strategic development efforts. Representation of the collective interests of universities was under the Vice Chancellors, Ghana (VCG, formerly the Committee of Vice-Chancellors and Principals), which has focused on negotiating stable conditions of service for its members. General policies and processes affecting university growth, educational policy and political governance have not been emphasized in the VCG's mandate. Yet considerable goodwill towards universities exists among government, the private sector and civil society leaders.

Members of Parliament shaping government policies claimed that university leadership simply ignores them[14] and that they intervene

[14] Source: statements and sentiments recorded during separate meetings with the Parliamentary Select Committee on Education and further expressions during the stakeholder validation workshop on the findings of the study.

in university matters only during crises and conflicts of interest. They do, however, remain eager to support university transformation as part of national development efforts. Members of government institutions responsible for institutional renewal lament that the best transformation proposals still await the kind of strategic leadership that is capable of framing and implementing such reforms.[15]

Non-governmental organizations and bilateral donors have had a few successes in establishing collaborative arrangements for development and poverty reduction with specific departments and units of Ghanaian universities. UNICEF's association with the Centre for Social Policy Studies at the University of Ghana and its funding of the Nutrition Centre at the University for Development Studies are good examples of innovations that could be transformed into new paradigms for teaching, learning and research. In spite of these successes, many more of these agencies are still looking for opportunities to work closely with universities seeking to address national poverty and development issues in Ghana.[16]

Student leadership

The role of student leadership in the transformation of universities was discussed at length in the preparation of this study.

Since 2000, student governance has seen considerable reform, with the introduction of a new constitution for the National Union of Ghana Students (NUGS), requiring the election of officers at a national congress of delegates from Student Representative Councils (SRCs) of the publicly funded universities. Hitherto NUGS officers were elected by designated campuses on a rotational basis, making the organization less representative of its full membership. With this new system, delegates of local NUGS chapters are elected on each campus and, together with the SRCs, represent their university at NUGS annual congresses. A national secretariat of NUGS, governed by an executive council, has been established to implement congress decisions. Its day-to-day functions are regulated by various commissions, prominent among which is the Women's Commission. A

[15] Evidence of this is recorded in meetings with staff of the National Institutional Renewal Programme (NIRP).
[16] Meetings with the Danish International Development Agency (DANIDA) suggested that overtures to university departments to develop courses related to poverty reduction have frequently been frustrated.

121

co-ordinating secretary, appointed for a one-year term, often as national service personnel, heads the secretariat. However, the short tenure of members of the secretariat has led to short-term perspectives and policies.

At individual campuses, student governance institutions are making modest transitions from a politics of rhetoric and confrontation to one of mobilizing student resources as a means of influencing investment decisions. The KNUST SRC, for example, is raising funds for a major housing complex, while the SRC at the University of Ghana has opened a student services centre. These efforts notwithstanding, the process of funding student governance has not been vigorous, and systems for managing student resources remain largely undeveloped. The main efforts have focused on fund-raising from external sources, rather than from students' own financial and labour resources. No jobs have been created by students, despite sharp decreases in services such as cleaning, catering, residence, libraries, games and recreation, among others. All of these services, previously offered free of charge by the university, have either been abolished or are woefully under-funded. Student leaders have not taken advantage of this opportunity to provide these services. Working in such campus service areas would provide students who tend to see themselves as part of an emerging elite with an opportunity to experience manual and cognitive labour as complementary rather than hierarchical. Given the difficult financial conditions of many students, working in the above-mentioned areas on campus could provide an ideal way of generating income through activities from which the university at large would benefit. There is the need for student leadership to deliberate with university authorities on the development of such job opportunities.

Student leadership has evolved considerably from the 1970s and 1980s when, through political and educational activities, it made major contributions to national development. Present student leadership is focused almost exclusively on social welfare issues, including whether and what to pay for. This orientation has kept them in conflict with university administrations and blocked their co-operation on issues of vital importance to both parties. One major casualty has been in the area of 'who pays for education, what is to be paid, and how'? There is also a perception that many students simply want to obtain their degrees and migrate out of Ghana, captured in the statement quoted in Chapter 1 that 'Medical students are writing their exams with their tickets in their pockets'.

This reflects both the pervasiveness of migration in the Ghanaian psyche and the reality of the brain drain for a global market (see Black et al., 2003). Thus, student futures are not seen as necessarily aligned with national priorities and needs, and their present predicaments as students may not therefore elicit the requisite sympathy. Universities thus have an opportunity to develop and introduce courses and programmes as well as to nurture leadership at different levels to produce a nationally oriented student body. These graduates would ideally commit themselves to using the knowledge gained through their education to solve problems of poverty and under-development in the local economy.

Strategic planning:
visions & perspectives of change

This study began by defining the components of university trans-formation that would be most relevant to Ghana. Transformation, whatever its form or origin, can be enhanced through deliberate management effort. The universities take seriously the use of strategic planning as a management tool. Those institutions without strategic plans are drawing them up for their institutions. Beyond that, the National Council for Tertiary Education (NCTE) is encouraging all institutions to adopt these management tools.

The use of strategic planning in universities is only a recent phenomenon. In the case of public universities in Ghana, it dates back to the mid-1990s. A detailed discussion of strategic planning in selected African universities is found in Ekong and Plante (1996). Comparing and critiquing the different plans would be a useful exercise in evaluating 'best practices' for strategic planning.

Strategic planning can be defined as an on-going effort to seek competitive advantage in the achievement of institutional goals. It is usually described in three basic steps:

- where are we now? (including the question of who we are)
- where would we like to be within the next few years?
- how do we get there?

123

Strategic planning emphasizes competitive advantage, whereas conventional planning 'tends to be oriented toward looking at problems based on current understanding, or an inside-out mindset. Strategic planning requires an understanding of the nature of the issue, and the finding of an appropriate response, or an outside-in mind set' (Rowley et al., 1997).

In addition, as noted in CSUN (1997):

Long-range planning is a projection from the present or an extrapolation from the past. Strategic planning builds on anticipated future trends, data, and competitive assumptions. Long-range planning tends to be numbers driven. Strategic planning tends to be idea driven, more qualitative; it seeks to provide a clear organizational vision/focus.

Beyond this, there are also differences between strategic planning in a business setting as compared with that in a university. Some of these differences, as stated by Lerner (1999), are:

- Time frame: businesses usually have a time frame of two–three years because of the products they offer. In the university, the minimum is about five years.
- Consensus: There is a need in universities to involve all the major constituents from the start, as they need to 'capture the vision' and thus be more able to help with implementation. This is important because strategic planning begins with strategic thinking.
- Value system: Public universities are interested in the long-term advancement of knowledge, and they are guided by the public interest. As is well-known, the normative underpinnings of tertiary education do not permit a reduction to mere economic efficiency, and effectiveness and inclusive deliberation are equally important values.
- Customers: In the case of universities, stakeholders or beneficiaries are not as narrow as in the case of a business customer base, and include students, society, employers and government, requiring more factors to be considered in planning.
- Context: Change does not occur easily in universities, since their very essence is about preservation, both of knowledge and social concerns.

After reviewing strategic plans at the University of Ghana (two plans) (UG, 1992; 2001), KNUST (KNUST, 2001) and UCC (UCC, 2000), we offer the following suggestions for improvement:

- It is essential for universities to share their strategic planning experiences and their different approaches.
- The experience of sharing will contribute to a common under-standing of terms such as *vision, mission, key thrusts, strategies* and *objectives.*
- Much is to be gained from collaboration with other universities in strategic planning.
- Universities should develop the institutional capacity for gathering and analyzing information on a continuous basis so that strategic plans are enriched and extended, to expand their scope.
- Because of current funding constraints, strategies tend to focus on resources to the detriment of teaching, programme research and extension. In this respect, the KNUST plan contains more refer-ences to specific teaching, research and public service strategies than those of the other two universities. Examples of such references include the following:

  - train high-level personnel in science and technology to support the industrial and socio-economic development of Ghana and Africa in a sustainable and environmentally friendly manner;
  - train highly qualified personnel for the development of the polytechnics and other tertiary institutions;
  - initiate new programmes and research to address public concerns about industry and rural communities;
  - encourage collaborative research with industry and the private sector and strengthen those links with other educational institutions.

Leadership for strategic planning

The role of the VCG

The Committee of Vice-Chancellors (CVC) was established in 1965 by the three extant publicly funded universities. By 1994, it had become the Committee of Vice-Chancellors and Principals (CVCP), after including the University College of Education, Winneba and the

University for Development Studies. In 2004, it changed its name to the Vice Chancellors, Ghana (VCG).

The VCG is a consultative body and a forum for discussing matters of common interest, but with no legal or statutory backing. The results of its deliberations are only recommendations to the governing councils of the individual universities. Over the years, its activities have covered the following areas:

- consultative meetings with the various staff associations/unions on conditions of service;
- levels of government subvention;
- specific matters referred to the universities for advice or comment;
- negotiations with appropriate parties in times of crisis, such as shutdowns;
- harmonization of academic fees;
- consultations with NUGS;
- international linkages;
- joint Superannuation Management Committee (this seems to have become redundant);
- management of the Universities of Ghana Overseas Office in the UK;
- staff training and development, to serve university goals.

The VCG has certainly been a champion of the publicly funded universities. It may be time, however, to define more clearly its role and functions. The VCG might be well advised to consider the following issues:

- providing opportunities for university heads to deliberate on matters of mutual concern;
- studying the problems and needs of universities, especially in their relations with other educational institutions, the government and society;
- collecting and disseminating information about their universities;
- promoting public confidence in the quality of the universities' efforts.

As the highest consultative body for public universities, the VCG has a unique opportunity to introduce and discuss system-wide issues affecting the institutions.

126

The role of the NCTE

The NCTE, as the successor to the National Council on Higher Education, was set up in 1993 under PNDC Law 454 as a buffer between educational institutions and the government. It plays an advisory role in policy-making and has budgetary and financial responsibilities. It is also charged with providing reliable information, vision and direction for the tertiary sector. However, the council does not have the staff necessary to carry out its functions. It has only recently recruited a budget analyst and a planning officer and still needs the services of a research and policy analyst, an ICT specialist and a publications officer. It is in discussions with the World Bank about strengthening the secretariat and the universities' management system.

The NCTE has recently begun several initiatives to strengthen governance structures in tertiary institutions. It has adapted the training manual for council members developed by the steering committee of the Working Group on Higher Education (WGHE) of the Association for the Development of Education in Africa (ADEA) to conditions in Ghana (NCTE, 2002). It has also developed a manual on conflict resolution and management skills and organized training for council members in universities and polytechnics (Effah and Mensah-Bonsu, 2001). It is also preparing a manual to help in understanding the budget cycle.

According to its executive secretary, the NCTE needs to plan ahead and to flag issues for the Minister of Education. It has commissioned studies in order to advise the government, instead of reacting to issues after the fact. It has also made a request to the Carnegie Corporation to fund annual major stakeholder meetings on a specific policy issue. The NCTE has furthermore set up a technical committee on the development of a strategic plan for higher education in Ghana.

9 Gender in the Institutions

Gender is a systemic component of all educational studies, since transformation in education, as in any other social realm, cannot proceed without engaging with issues of gender equity. Existing studies on gender in universities have focused mainly on the levels of participation of females and males in various sectors (cf. Prah, 2003). As a centre for educational leadership and knowledge creation, the university is in a good position to provide leadership in gender equity: first in the example it sets, and secondly in the direction it gives through research findings and outreach programmes.

In meetings with the university authorities in Ghana, gender did not seem to be a conscious issue on their agendas. The public universities in Ghana have no gender policy, and their policy frameworks are not attuned to gender concerns. While national discourse since the mid-1980s has shown a general commitment to gender equity and varying degrees of commitment to its inclusion in national policy processes (Tsikata, 2001), this subject has not engaged the attention of Ghanaian universities, which pay little attention to gender issues and inequalities. One exception to this is the new UCC strategic plan (UCC, 2000), which makes references to gender, albeit without developing any strategies to address it. Thus the UCC has yet to prove that the reference to gender is not just lip-service to a concept that is in vogue in developmental discourse, but that it demonstrates a real commitment to equity in social and political relations on campus. In general, universities have paid little attention to gender issues. However, as one Vice-Chancellor stated, 'one may be doing a lot, but without a conscious policy. On the other hand, one can have the existence of policies, and yet do nothing.' Another respondent from the UCC remarked that the university had problems 'more pressing than gender'! Given the leadership role of African public universities, the passive nature of their engagement with issues so critical to the prospects for Africa's development (Palmer, 1991; Manuh, 1998) is a matter for concern. While universities have not waited for the government's guidance in other areas, one Vice-Chancellor suggested that the lack of a national gender policy was the reason for the universities' complacence on this issue.

Interviews with top administrators revealed that the core values of the university revolve around its main activities of research, teaching, administration and extension. The ethics that guide teaching are the integrity of lecturers, confidentiality, fairness, quality assurance, relations with students and academic professionalism. Among the primary research concerns are intellectual property rights and plagiarism, the integrity of research, the ethics of data collection and the reporting of research findings. There is also the issue of maintaining the integrity of the university, such as through the promotion of academic staff by the use of external assessments. Here, quality must be assured by selecting good assessors and evaluating their assessments. A core value in administration is fairness to all irrespective of background, sex, religion, etc. However, given the clear regulations for recruitment, promotion and placement, some groups, including women, do not meet the set standards. In the matter of appointments, for example, there are no concerns about ensuring gender balance, and the only criterion used is the applicant's qualifications. In the extension work of universities, the stated goal is to make an impact on communities. But there has been little conscious effort to relate these core values to the promotion of gender equity in the universities or to the achievement of gender equality in Ghanaian society.

As sites of production and dissemination of knowledge, universities are confronted with the problem of hegemonic knowledge that marginalizes other perspectives and methodologies. The ensuing epistemic injustice in the area of gender-related institutional practices and gender-sensitive or gender-centred approaches to knowledge production also needs to be addressed in both institutional arrangements and the curriculum.

The policy environment & gender

From the interviews and opinions expressed, it appears that attention to gender concerns arises from university traditions and not from policy or extant structures. These traditions in turn depend on personalities and on the beliefs and perceptions they bring to their office. The implications of this for governance and the pursuit of the core values of the university should be addressed. In discussions with key administrators, much was made of the personality of Vice-

Chancellors and other leaders in creating a gender-sensitive environment. There was considerable talk of 'encouraging' senior women through personal interaction, and of the need to publish their research for career advancement, but there was no formalized structure for this or for monitoring its effectiveness. While enlightened leadership is commended, the danger of leaving gender equity to the goodwill of a leader cannot be overstressed. Respondents in leadership positions spoke about 'encouraging females' and expected women in positions of leadership to help 'the others'. Many respondents blamed women themselves, saying that 'women are their worst enemies' and that 'females in leadership positions tended to be harder on their own sex'. The promotion of gender equity is not seen as an institutional concern or as an expression of power relations that are deeply contested by both males and females. 'Once you are a lecturer, you are a lecturer. One closes his [sic] eyes to the gender issue', commented one Vice-Chancellor.

There is thus a clear need for gender-related policies to ensure that gender equity is a value upheld in academia. Except in its discursive use in the UCC Strategic Plan mentioned above, the promotion of gender equity is not identified as an objective in the strategic plan of any of the institutions or in the work of the NCTE, beyond the goal of increasing the proportion of female students. In turn, this goal is not linked to any specific output or national objective. The absence of institutional policies on issues of gender equity at the universities is simply remarkable. Equal opportunity units, sexual harassment policies or grievance procedures do not exist in any of the institutions. University leaders hide under statements such as the following: 'there is a non-discrimination clause in the Constitution', 'the university consciously does not discriminate', 'we have a disciplinary committee', in order to justify their inaction. While complaints about sexual harassment on campuses come up repeatedly, no university has yet developed a policy against these offences, and few allegations are ever fully investigated or substantiated. Judging by their record, Ghanaian public universities are extremely old-fashioned in their disregard for gender equity. They are failing to provide leadership to other institutions or in the national arena, despite the fact that gendered violence is on the increase and that national authorities have set up a Women and Juvenile Unit (WAJU) within the police service to deal with violence and abuse against women and children.

In the recent review of its statutes in 2003, the University of Ghana was encouraged to extend its non-discrimination clause to all female members of the university community beyond female students, as previously stated. The university council has now been charged with creating a nurturing environment for all its constituent members, with due attention to gender, disability, race and ethnicity, *inter alia*. The university has gone ahead to create the position of a Pro-Vice-Chancellor for Operations, Development and Diversity, thus theoretically opening up the space for recognition and respect of different forms of diversity including dis/ability, sexual orientation and sexual identity and other combinations of stigmatized categories that are not just additional but bring out the special experiences of marginalization/discrimination that need to be acknowledged. Thus more research, especially on the experience of dis/abled students, is needed to provide a platform to identify their needs, which can then be translated into policies fostering integrated higher education.

Female enrolment in the universities

The main area of universities' engagement with gender equity has been in the realm of educational access. Yet, as noted in Chapter 5, it is possible to increase access without improving equity. More female representation, especially in student enrolments, may only reinforce the class and location inequities in Ghanaian society. In all universities, the female proportion of total enrolment has indeed increased. At the University of Ghana, the proportion of female students rose from 23 per cent in 1990 to 38 per cent in 2001. According to the Vice-Chancellor, it will not be long before parity is achieved. Similarly, at the UCC, female enrolment has risen from 20 per cent in 1990 to 27 per cent in 2001 (UG, 2002a; UCC, 2002). The current trend is towards higher female representation at the senior secondary school (SSS) level as well. However, as Akyeampong et al. (1998) noted, the improvement in female enrolment rates at the SSS level might have been the result of an increase in male drop-out rates. The rise in female tertiary enrolment rates is occurring simultaneously with a decline in overall SSS enrolments, in particular of males. Table 24 shows the enrolment of boys and girls in basic and senior secondary schools.

131

Table 24: Boys' & girls' enrolment in primary, junior and senior secondary schools, 1991–2001

Year	Primary		JSS		SSS	
	Boys	Girls	Boys	Girls	Boys	Girls
1991/92	985,747	821,476	349,080	243,787	150,740	74,537
1992/93	1,003,742	844,558	365,934	263,324	164,623	82,873
1993/94	1,034,394	876,014	379,008	276,634	154,927	81,603
1994/95	1,035,348	885,455	377,317	282,534	130,446	71,367
1995/96	1,051,306	904,407	384,855	292,786	122,070	72,015
1996/97	1,087,718	939,465	391,763	303,705	115,881	73,027
1997/98	1,066,278	933,562	394,083	310,333	118,033	74,383
1998/99	1,097,670	963,074	403,293	325,983	121,588	76,624
1999/00	1,123,394	991,587	405,486	330,765	117,275	87,351
2000/01	1,067,686	954,282	382,809	316,544	n.a.	n.a.

Source: Ghana Education Service, 2002.

Overall trends in female enrolment at university show increases, as seen in Figure 7 for the UCC.

While in all the public universities an unofficial affirmative action policy gives some preference to females meeting the minimum admission requirements, a closer examination of applications and admissions data reveals that this policy may not be fully honoured. There are other structural factors impeding female enrolments, since the proportion of qualified female applicants subsequently admitted ought to be higher than it currently is. This situation accentuates the need for clear guidelines to ensure the effectiveness of this policy.

Not surprisingly, there was concern expressed by some respondents that affirmative action tended to weaken women's fight for equality, since it is viewed as an admission of weakness on the part of females. Such respondents would prefer females to be given better preparation for university entry. At the UCC, remedial classes in science are now offered to help students meet the minimum entry requirements in that field. While such classes do not target females specifically, interviews showed that these classes have given females more opportunity to gain admission to science programmes where female representation is lowest.

In line with these admission trends, the universities have increased their residential accommodation available to women. In the older universities, three male halls were built, on average, before

132

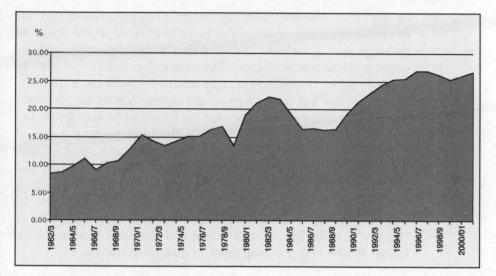

%

Source: UCC, 2002a, 2002b.

Figure 7: Trends in female enrolment at UCC, 1962/3–2001/2

the first residence hall for females was constructed. Legon, Akuafo and Commonwealth Halls (for men) at the University of Ghana were constructed before Volta Hall (female) was constructed. Similarly at KNUST, Queen's, Independence and Republic Halls existed before Africa Hall was available for females. Now, with the exception of Volta and Commonwealth Halls at the University of Ghana, University Hall (male) and Africa Hall at KNUST, and Casely-Hayford (male) and Adehye (female) Halls at the UCC, all the other halls are mixed, and there is an unwritten general policy to give a slight preference to females in these residential facilities. However, the universities need to target the same percentage of spaces for males and females in all mixed halls.

The attention to females and to gender balance is not applied consistently. As one registrar noted, on a very simple test of 'how many toilet facilities are there for females in your institution?' most universities would be hard pressed to produce the numbers and their indications of progress towards gender equity. Indeed, in discussions with university administrators, gender did not appear to be a factor

133

in planning. Similarly, only in recent physical development on campuses are issues of disabilities being considered in the design of buildings and amenities. The fact that some university facilities might prove uncomfortable or unfriendly to females did not seem to occur to many respondents in administrative positions. To be fair, some attention has been given to improving lighting for increased security, but this was often done for the benefit of foreign, fee-paying students. Lighting is certainly one of the most reactive gendered interventions in security, as discourses construct darkness as a quasi-legitimate space for the perpetrators of crime. Gendered security has to be much more proactive, and security has to be guaranteed all over campus, at all times, and especially at times of power failure. In addition, security staff need to be sensitized about issues of gendered violence, and the dynamics of shame and guilt that tend to silence female victims and grant impunity to male perpetrators.

Female representation among academic & professional staff

Female representation among academic and professional staff is fairly low in all institutions. While career paths tend to be continuous for males, those of females are often interrupted by considerations of family life. By the time a female acquires a master's degree she may be 30 years old. Thus, even if more females enter universities, they may not necessarily advance sufficiently to become university teachers, in light of the demands for terminal degrees. There are no targets for females in postgraduate admissions nor are there explicit policies to encourage their recruitment and training, although they may be favoured informally. Thus, at KNUST, UCC and UG, attempts were made to ensure that females were nominated for positions or training, but nominations did not always lead to appointments. There were also some reported attempts to give priority to women in the area of staff development. However, as in the case of graduate studies and training institutions, it is not likely that there will be equitable female representation in the staff of universities in the near future.

As a result, there are few women in top leadership positions in Ghanaian universities, with the exception of KNUST where the registrar and university librarian are females, and at the UCC where

Table 25: KNUST staff by category and gender

Staff Category	Female	Male	Total	% Female
Junior staff	317	1459	1776	17.8
Senior staff	165	338	503	32.8
Senior members	61	618	679	8.98
Professors (full) & equivalent	2	9	11	18.2
Associate Professors & equivalent	5	41	46	10.87
Senior lecturers & equivalent	10	160	170	5.88
Lecturers & equivalent	44	408	452	9.73

Source: KNUST Statistics, 2002.

Table 26: UG staff by category and gender

Staff Category	Female	Male	Total	% Female
Junior staff	425	2239	2664	16.0
Senior staff	283	647	930	30.4
Senior members	186	739	925	20.1
Professors (full) & equivalent	4	52	56	7.1
Associate professors & equivalent	9	79	88	10.2
Senior lecturers & equivalent	43	203	246	17.5
Lecturers & equivalent	98	342	440	22.3

Source: UG, 2004.

the finance officer is a woman. Among deans, the only females at present are the dean of the UCC faculty of arts and the dean of the UG faculty of agriculture. The University of Ghana elected a female Pro-Vice-Chancellor in 1996 who is noted for her proactivism on behalf of female students and staff. At KNUST, there were six female heads of department at the time of the survey. Representation of females throughout the professoriate is very low, and, typically, fewer female faculty members have terminal degrees. Table 25 shows the current distribution of staff by category and gender at KNUST. As shown in the table, females make up only 9 per cent of senior members. In contrast, females are about 20 per cent of senior members at the University of Ghana (UG, 2004). Senior members, however, also include both academic and administrative staff, and actual numbers of female teaching and research staff in both institutions are fewer.

135

Since representation on university boards and committees is often based on the position held in departments, faculties, schools or institutes, and because few women are in these positions, they are under-represented in the decision-making structures. The university does not waive such criteria in favour of females, nor does it make conscious efforts to give females fair representation even on *ad hoc* bodies where representation is by nomination or voting by an appointing entity. Thus, at the University of Cape Coast, boards such as the University Consultative Council, the Research and Conferences Committee, the Board of Survey and the School of Agriculture Board, had no female members at the time of our study. On the other hand, boards and committees chaired by females, such as the Board of the Faculty of Arts, the Kindergarten Board, the Basic Schools Management Committee and the Superannuation Management Board, have the highest number of female members. With the exception of the Basic Schools Management Committee, which has a female membership of seven, the rest have three women each. On the Academic Board of KNUST, there were 12 females (out of a total membership of 114), consisting of the registrar, the librarian, four professors and six heads of department.

Gender & the place of women in the institutions

A disturbing finding on gender in the institutions is its instrumentalization. In response to a question on the absence of gender in strategic plans, one Vice-Chancellor noted that it was submerged, but that he would want to see it flagged *if* it could attract funds.

Statements about what faculty women in leadership positions at the University of Ghana, for instance, have achieved over the past five years reinforce a fear of instrumentalization. The construction of a permanent building, complete with a library, for the Faculty of Law and new buildings for the Institute of African Studies, have both occurred under female leadership and are indeed commendable, but gender equity ought to be pursued for more reasons than the resources women are able to attract to their institutions.

More generally, some respondents said that the socio-cultural environment during the 1960s and '70s was so hostile to women that it did not encourage 'brainy' women to emerge at the top of classes. In contrast, the social environment is seen as more supportive

136

now, with female achievers in a number of areas who are seen as role models for the younger generation. It is still not clear, however, how far these female 'achievers' challenge gender-related social norms or whether high female achievement levels are compatible with these norms.

Female respondents spoke of generally held perceptions that men worked harder than women, who were more likely to go on leave, including maternity leave. Furthermore, they observed that female staff were often given less challenging assignments that did not improve their skills. Worse, where women refused to play the domestic role at work (such as serving the tea), they were branded as arrogant.

Female participants in the focus group discussions at KNUST said that when they tried to improve themselves, they were seen as bossy and aggressive, and that there was often a social price to be paid for seeking promotion. There were also problems at the interpersonal level in terms of the way individuals saw women's position in society and its effect on their relationships with successful university women. Participants complained about the advice offered to success-ful academic women, suggesting more interest in their accomplish-ments as wives and mothers than as academics. Such women were often cautioned not to forget their domestic roles and their most important title of 'Mrs'. Respondents were told that this title was more important than their academic titles, and the insistence on inserting the marital title 'Mrs' in brackets alongside women's academic titles as in 'Dr. (Mrs)' appears to validate these concerns. On the other hand, it could also be argued that these insertions help to make female holders of academic titles visible, as the assumption still exists that a Doctor or Professor is likely to be male. However, unmarried women are unlikely to have a Ms. inserted after their doctoral or professorial titles.

While female faculty at the UCC felt that they were not silenced, those at KNUST – and to a lesser extent at UG – felt that they were subject to silencing practices through name calling, raising of voices and the personalization of any issues raised by a woman. Women at the University of Ghana pointed out that many people believe that discrimination does not exist, even as men dominate women (overtly or covertly), which makes silencing very difficult to challenge. Others complained about specific issues such as the claim that childcare is the concern only of women, or the practice of using titles such as 'Doctor' or 'Professor' for men, while women are often only called 'Mrs' even when they are professors or hold doctorates. Some women added that when they refuse certain roles such as introducing chairpersons or giving a vote of thanks that are often relegated to females, they are labelled as 'unco-operative'.

Sexual cultures & relationships

High levels of transactional sex seem to be endemic on all campuses at all levels, with students derisively referring to 'sexually trans-mitted grades' where male academic staff take sexual advantage of female students in exchange for high marks. Another case of harass-ment involves the practice known as 'protocol student' or concessionary admissions that fall outside the normal selection criteria, where sexual favours may be required for admission. The specific cases mentioned included:

- male lecturers and teaching assistants pressuring female students for sex in return for higher grades;
- male clerical staff being approached by female students to alter their grades in return for sexual favours;
- female students offering sex to lecturers in return for higher grades.

Sexual corruption is not limited to Ghanaian campuses, as is shown in papers presented in the panel on 'Gender and Higher Education' at the Women's World Congress in Kampala in July 2002 (see Pereira, 2002). Such behaviour arises partly from insecurities in national life and the resulting need to ensure personal advancement by whatever means.

Our interviews suggested that female students seldom reported these incidents, and that some of those who did refused to identify their harassers or to testify before a committee of enquiry. The dean of students' affairs at the UCC stated that only one incident of sexual harassment had been reported to his office, but that it had been withdrawn before he could take any disciplinary action. According to student informants, students expressed fear of victimization by their harassers or stigmatization by others who would blame the victim and not the harasser. Instead, students preferred to report these experiences to their religious groups and friends who might be more empathetic and likely to keep the confidence entrusted to them. These issues need to be borne in mind when grievance bodies are established on campuses.

Another source of stress for females lies in their relations with male students. Generally, such relations were reportedly cordial on an individual basis, but too often groups of men were less friendly. These situations occur in the lecture halls, in student politics and through group mobbing and harassment of females, especially by members of all-male halls. Female students identified Commonwealth Hall (UG) and Casely-Hayford Hall (UCC) as particularly problematic. Many male students complained about too-provocative female clothing as sexually arousing and thus harassing. Some halls of residence have 'traditions' restricting the colour of clothes females should wear to enter these halls: females who wear red clothing in some of these halls are often jeered at and harassed.

Many female students are traumatized by this experience, while residents see it as 'just having fun'. In other halls, females who dress 'provocatively' are 'brought to order', indicating the collective power of men over women. Interestingly, male students are often seen with non-student females in no less 'provocative' outfits than those they complain about, suggesting that the issue is really about control. This is further supported by the fact that male students wear net shirts (referred to as 'air conditioned') and other transparent or flamboyant clothes that would be considered 'inappropriate' if worn by women.

Female students also report abuse in the lecture hall from their male peers. Women who speak up in class are given names such as *Obaa dindin*, 'hard female,' to silence them. 'The guys will say, "hey! You are *too* know, sit down, shut up", all those things' (Focus group discussion with female students, KNUST, July 2002).

No gender regulations on harassment or discrimination exist at universities, but many respondents believed they were needed. Other recommendations from respondents were that:

- a special body should be set up to deal with sexual harassment;
- structures for handling cases of sexual harassment should be made known to all;

- orientation for new employees should cover sexual harassment and rights;
- a brochure on sexual harassment should be developed and widely distributed;
- sanctions for harassers should include dismissal for students and staff, or, at the least, loss of salary or office space. Senior staff found guilty of sexual harassment should lose their titles and be dismissed;
- a sexual reproductive service centre for students supported by telephone hotlines is needed;
- affairs between departmental staff and their subordinates should not be tolerated. (From statements made in the focus group discussions, it appeared that female junior staff do not feel that they are free to accept or reject the overtures of their bosses);
- the low representation of females in student politics should be addressed.

Many female students appeared less interested in social issues, and some male students seemed to resent the fact that the SRC has a special women's commission. Their comments suggested that they saw this commission as having two conflicting goals – to be independent of the SRC at the same time as it benefited from its financial/political support. While women students felt that the women's commission should be more proactive, students generally were less optimistic about women's chances in student elections. The fact that certain 'soft' positions – such as treasurer or vice-president – are on occasion reserved for women would also appear to impede their accession to the presidency of either the Junior Common Room or the SRC. At both UCC and KNUST, men agreed that: 'For a woman to take up a higher position she must be like a man.'

From the above, it is clear that institutional changes are needed to empower women within the existing misogynistic campus cultures. There is a need for women's offices where female students can report discrimination confidentially or obtain support in a nurturing environment to break the gendered imposition of guilt and shame that silences female victims. Such spaces can also offer support for learning and career advancement and gender-related research and projects, to demonstrate the salience of gender and the necessity of a gender-sensitive approach to help females thrive in

140

academia. Instead of the present situation where some females do such jobs gratuitously and without recognition, the university needs to appoint gender-sensitive women and men to serve in such positions.

Gender in the curricula

In response to questions about courses on gender in the university curriculum, a Vice-Chancellor stated that their availability was the responsibility of departments and up to the relevant boards and committees. The explanation given for this position is that universities must avoid the danger of 'just taking a bit of a discipline that cannot stand the test of time'. He added a caution about resources and the tendency of special programmes to grow. However, these views are contradicted by the experience with gender-related courses at the Institute of African Studies, where the two courses on gender are the most popular optional subjects in the M.A./M.Phil. programme.

According to a student from the UCC, 'the university hasn't got any programme or literature on gender'. At the UCC, the Vice-Chancellor stated that all departments had been asked to build gender into their curriculum by 2002, but that it was not possible to ascertain their compliance with this directive.

Several courses on gender are offered at both the UCC and the University of Ghana, but KNUST had no courses at the time of our survey. At the UCC, sixteen such courses were identified – five at the graduate level and another five in the final undergraduate year but some students were sceptical about access to these courses. In the final year, course offerings are restricted to fewer students; only three courses were open to first-year students and only one was available to second-year students, a particular concern for the small numbers of students starting at this level. No gender-related courses were offered in the School of Agriculture or the Faculties of Education and Science. The lack of gender courses in Education is particularly troubling as many of its graduates go into teaching; gender awareness should be a part of their pedagogical training if gender equity and equality are to be national goals.

At the University of Ghana, over 20 courses on gender and women's studies are offered in the Faculties of Arts, Law, Social

141

Studies and Agriculture. In the Faculty of Agriculture, the courses are offered through the Home Science Department. Many of the courses are graduate-level optional subjects based on demand and the availability of resources. None are core courses, and there are no gender programmes in Science.

Courses were identified only from titles, and not by content, and the extent to which academic planning committees have encouraged them is unclear. Yet national needs for qualified graduates in this subject are hard to overstate, particularly with respect to advancing equitable economic development.

Students, staff and faculty seem to favour gender-related courses. At the University of Ghana, students wanted these courses to be a core part of their curriculum and to be offered in the first year. Faculty members also asked for training in gender analysis during their long vacation. They were also of the opinion that the university should include gender issues in the basic curriculum and that the orientation of new faculty members ought to include issues such as sexual harassment and gender policy.

Resources for gender studies

There is no place in university budgets for gender education, and the universities offer no direct resources. Instead, programmes on gender have relied on NGOs or external contacts initiated in different departments, centres and institutes. Ghanaian universities in general have no funded research or extension activities in gender and women's studies, although both female and male academics do work and have interests in this area on their own initiative, without any institutional direction or support. As one female administrator observed, the research interests of staff are self-determined without direction from above, and are more constrained by the availability of funds.

Gender-relevant publications emerging from such research cover such areas as food-processing technologies, gender relations in educational institutions, literary works by women, gender issues in religion, health and reproductive decision-making, labour, work and employment issues, women's rights, the state, gender and policy, access to resources and political participation, and trade and economic policy-making. Moreover, much of this work is pro-actively aimed at influencing government choices affecting local and global gender relations.

The interview sessions also raised the gender awareness of some male respondents about the gender relevance of university policy. Some said that participation in the present study had offered them a fresh experience of looking at the university with a gendered eye. The study thereby advanced the issue of gender in the university setting and laid the groundwork for taking it further. Although institutionalizing gender into university culture is a massive undertaking calling for new resources and skills, policy changes, sufficient funding and the evolution of attitudes against deep-seated prejudice and practices, along with a shift in power relations, these impediments can be overcome with the support of the university authorities in a process of transformation. The necessary adjustments, however, entail a paradigm shift on the part of social, political and educational leaders towards the goal of improving life for all Ghanaian citizens equally by acknowledging and addressing inequities wherever they appear.

10 Challenges, Lessons & Recommendations

In this concluding chapter, we review the salient challenges, the responses that they have evoked and the lessons that they have for public universities and for society in general in Ghana. The study examined complexities in Ghanaian higher education and their socio-political context. These complexities have conditioned choices and shaped the directions of change. The extent and willingness of universities to move beyond routine ways of acting to forge linkages with industry, government and communities will determine the pace of change in the transformation from poverty to increased well-being and improved human capabilities for the broad majority of Ghanaians.

The first challenges are those triggered by the context of change, including the prevailing policies and practices in the wider political economy, while the second challenge refers to internal dynamics in universities.

Complexity of the reform context

As is well known, Ghana adhered strongly to structural adjustment programmes during the mid-1980s and early 1990s. A myriad of IMF-led social policy reforms was implemented, while the World Bank and other donors financed many projects, particularly in the sector of Ghanaian exports. The crippling burden of national debt that ensued has now been replaced by stringent austerity. A negative feature of these macroeconomic reforms has been a drift away from higher education as a public priority towards basic education, and an ethos of 'structural adjustment' in university education, defined by an emphasis on institutional rationalization, cost-recovery and market-response planning. Universities have thus become preoccupied with extreme adversity as cutbacks in funding have been simultaneous with growing demand, leaving them with little latitude for innovation or transformation.

With the exception of Sawyerr (1994, 2002), little work has been done to understand the policy implications of this era for universities and other Ghanaian institutions of higher education. Research is still needed to chronicle and understand the reforms and their ongoing cultural and economic impact on Ghana.

The lesson for university leaders is that higher education planning and management are constrained by economic concerns and political choices, in particular by the hegemonic consequences of SAPs. A better understanding of these effects is imperative for the universities.

Growing poverty & the role of universities

Deepening poverty has been one of the impacts of SAPs in Ghana. In university education, although enrolments are rising, admissions from poorer regions and schools have declined drastically, as more competitive entry requirements favour students from wealthier regions and schools. The government has responded with a poverty reduction strategy and programme, but these are directed mostly at the symptoms instead of the roots of poverty. Growing exclusion of the poor from educational opportunities and tighter funding constraints in higher education were reviewed in Chapter 3. There have been many useful advances, some of which have been detailed above, but the absence of any unified leadership by the universities on these subjects has served to perpetuate many aspects of the poverty problem. Strategies and solutions exist, but they need to be articulated, developed and taught by the universities to be effective for the transformation needed in Ghanaian society. Universities should and can become beacons of knowledge linked to action.

Universities as social & political communities

Universities in Ghana, as elsewhere, are social and political communities linking men and women of different generations, backgrounds, opinions and capacities for social action. Their intellectual capabilities and diverse associations could be catalytic in mobilizing society for educational transformation. At the same time, African universities serve as a source for recruitment by governments – democratic and military alike. In Ghana, the pervasive influence of faculty members in government also places the university at the centre of public policy choice. As leading consultants for national and international agencies, university personnel and institutions are influential among potential sources of financial aid for education and other social priorities. Some former student leaders have also emerged as key players in the political process. However, universities have not been stolid defenders of the importance of higher education in national development.

This study has found a wide diversity of organizational patterns in university management, both co-operative and competitive. These include a workers' union (TEWU), the university teachers' association (UTAG), two associations of university administrators (GAUA and FUSSAG), student councils (SRCs) and the National Union of Ghanaian Students (NUGS). The VCG aspires to be an apex body for university administrative leadership. Too often these stakeholders are preoccupied with the 'bread and butter' issues of workers, students and university welfare and with their academic mandate. A perspective of the 'university as a system' embracing all of its parts was found mainly among the workers' unions in virtually all the universities and rarely elsewhere, revealing a need for larger perspectives on the universities' impact.[17] Little solidarity exists among the other political groups that might mobilize for social change in favour of educational goals, and university leaders should develop such a constituency.

Strategic leadership & drivers of change

University leadership has been diverted to crisis management during recent decades, due to ongoing resource concerns. Drastic cuts in public funding, decreasing returns on assets and a rising number of qualified applicants set against the shrinking capacity for increased enrolment have forced university management into a precarious subsistence strategy. Under siege, administrators suffer collective bargaining battles over conditions of service and over who pays for and gets what, when and how, with the attendant students, faculty and staff voicing unrest. Such conditions set aside strategic thinking in exchange for merely surviving terms of office just to keep pace with the pressures. Stakeholders – students, faculty and other staff – compete to 'serve' their constituencies by representing them in

[17] The fact that TEWU is a national union and part of the TUC also enables university workers to interact with and establish solidarity with other workers throughout the country.

allocations. Planning and leading a university in the service of social needs and transforming teaching, research and learning capacities towards this end are rarely possible in this setting.

The challenge of knowledge production

The university as a primary site for knowledge production and dissemination is threatened by increasing student numbers and teaching loads, inadequate staff, poor infrastructure and facilities, stagnant resources and the absence of focused devotion to practical policy issues. Increasing conflict over relevance, as some institutions strive for market-driven courses while others seek to implement their core mandate, has worsened this stagnation. While postgraduate training is seen as a key to knowledge production, no clear visions or resources for this endeavour have emerged. University libraries are under-funded, except for some sporadic collaboration initiatives within Africa and overseas. The renewal of university publishing has not kept pace with the rising demand for titles and journals for research and teaching. The universities have also been affected negatively by the creation of new centres of research and policy analysis, which have co-opted resources that might have traditionally come to them and reduced their control over policy issues.

The place of private universities

The rise of predominantly religious private universities reflects a growing religiosity in Ghanaian society and raises concerns about diversity, tolerance and free expression. In addition, the emergence of new institutions – with the nation's resources and teaching staff overextended and training of faculty under-funded – raises quality issues for all institutions.

The NCTE is concerned with the regulation and provision of incentives to private universities since, in its view, the stronger they become, the more resources are freed up for other priorities. The private universities are resistant to regulation, asserting that as start-ups they need to find their feet before they can assume any such obligations. They also desire access to GETFund for their financial support.

Despite these stresses, some lessons are evident. First, the increase in providers of university education has widened the range of educational choice. Second, more institutions are concerned now

147

about educational policy. Third, these new private universities represent another constituency of interests which wield potentially different influences on public policy processes from the public universities.[18] Consequently, whether they co-operate or compete with the public universities, they should ultimately bring more attention to university education than has been the case hitherto. The major challenge for these new entrants will lie in sharing resources with the public universities, while competing with their course offerings. A further issue is the broadening of the pool for recruitment of staff. At present, these new universities have drawn staff from the public universities. Strategies for graduate training, including collaborative funding for a new generation of faculty, are a major challenge for both types of institutions.

Challenges of integrating HIV-AIDS in university transformation

In view of its importance for national and human resource development, if not the continued survival of the university, there is an increasingly urgent need for university administrators to view HIV/AIDS not only as a public health issue for students, but also as a major threat to human resource capacity and to the management functions of universities, in which more leadership is needed. Universities must show compassion and courage by introducing courses on HIV/AIDS in their curricula, while encouraging more research on the impact of HIV/AIDS on university structures and management, as well as for national development objectives. University health systems will have to start tracking HIV/AIDS cases and design humane policies for infected staff and students, while fostering openness about the disease. This is a daunting challenge that universities need to face.

Centring gender in university transformation

The university is a gendered environment dominated by males, where female students, staff and faculty often experience hostile and

[18] Members of the Parliamentary Select Committee on Education, on a visit to the new Catholic University in Sunyani, commended the leadership on its efforts to bring university education to the poor. University leaders in turn brought up their special legislative and policy requirements. The Select Committee plans similar visits to other private universities.

148

Strategic plans need to be prioritised in terms of p on initiatives that have catalytic impacts with lon systemic change.

150

sexually threatening behaviour, as well as intellectual belittling and undervaluation. Few if any policies exist to guide gender relations on campuses, and the universities have failed to challenge sexism and gender discrimination. While many of these sexual practices reflect inequities in society and education that remain too often unquestioned, universities should be using their resources to remedy these violations, rather than to perpetuate them. Sexist attitudes should be addressed and policies introduced to foster respect in an egalitarian, nurturing environment for all. Universities need to adopt a more proactive approach to gender issues, setting targets and devising systems to monitor and report on their progress.

Universities should tie their policy efforts for gender balance in education to national goals not only for students, but also for faculty and other staff. More attention to equity issues of all kinds should help to ensure that advances do not benefit only the already advantaged, while explicit targeting of women in postgraduate training should narrow the gap in female representation throughout these institutions.

University academic planning committees should undergo training to integrate gender into course offerings and to organize seminars and other programmes for both faculty and staff. As proposed in the focus group discussions, universities must seek to raise public awareness on gender issues through community-outreach activities. Students suggested that universities should think of ways to enrol more women students in traditionally gendered disciplines. Finally, universities need to establish centres of gender studies to monitor and promote the mainstreaming of gender in the curricula and the implementation of gender equity policies. Centres and units to monitor and intervene in gender relations should be established in all Ghanaian universities, while special attention should be directed to the promotion of gender-inclusive language, the use of which should be compulsory for all teaching staff during seminars and lectures.

Recommendations

These recommendations are offered to assist universities in meeting the challenge of managing a difficult transformation involving the co-ordination of multiple elements of the educational enterprise to achieve their goals more effectively.

149

Designing change efforts

The transformation processes observed during the study suggest that careful planning is needed to bring about any successful change. This planning must be embedded into existing structures and procedures of decision-making, and implemented with the following four important considerations:

Designating the strategic planning team with appropriate institutional support

The practice whereby strategic planning efforts are assigned to a 'committee' and handled as routine tasks should be reviewed. In its place, teams should be composed of key university members with expertise in strategic planning and motivated by a vision extending beyond operational problems. Negotiating the strategic vision of the university with representatives of key stakeholders is an essential first step. Beyond that, the tasks to be accomplished should be clearly elaborated and the intended results specified. Strategic planning efforts must be engaged with adequate funding and institutional support in order to be completed successfully in a timely manner.

Extending the consultative and participatory nature of the process

Currently, strategic planning efforts have mainly involved consultations with members of the university. However, they need to expand to involve extensive consultations with relevant community members, especially those with a stake in the outcome. This process should include key segments of the public policy process, in particular Members of Parliament, leaders from the private sector, civil society groups and public institutions with a stake in the university or its various products. This broader scope of input should empower the university to develop a widely shared vision with its public, as well as to establish credible linkages that may yield more political and financial backing for its resulting endeavours and programmes.

Developing 'flagship' initiatives

Strategic plans need to be prioritized in terms of projects and to focus on initiatives that have catalytic impacts with long-term potential for systemic change.

150

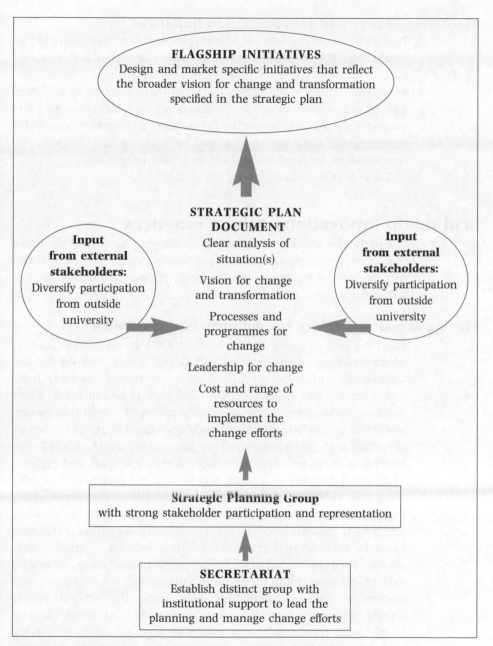

FLAGSHIP INITIATIVES
Design and market specific initiatives that reflect the broader vision for change and transformation specified in the strategic plan

Input from external stakeholders:
Diversify participation from outside university

STRATEGIC PLAN DOCUMENT
Clear analysis of situation(s)

Vision for change and transformation

Processes and programmes for change

Leadership for change

Cost and range of resources to implement the change efforts

Input from external stakeholders:
Diversify participation from outside university

Strategic Planning Group
with strong stakeholder participation and representation

SECRETARIAT
Establish distinct group with institutional support to lead the planning and manage change efforts

Figure 8: Designing and managing change and transformation efforts

151

Marketing change and transformation initiatives

Too often, the completion of a strategic plan has been restricted to 'marketing' the entire plan, where these rather bulky documents include no clearly defined projects. Marketing strategies for distinct initiatives should be developed to propel them from mere activities and timelines into dynamic proposals for specific change. Such strategies should incorporate the full range of stakeholders, especially private sector institutions, organized civil society and development organizations, as partners in their successful promotion.

These four steps are represented in Figure 8.

Scaling-up innovations & best practices

The particular innovations designed as 'flagship initiatives' are those that position the universities to serve society better, as they fulfil the core mandate of teaching, learning, research and community service. Suggested flagship initiatives are:

Moving access and equity beyond increased enrolment

The emerging example is the University for Development Studies, where reflective strategies for enhancing access and equity for traditionally vulnerable groups – such as women, students from poorer regions and disabled people – will need to be expanded. More systematic admissions access and equity strategies – such that gender and origin are no longer serious handicaps – must be promoted across all public and private universities. Since 2002/2003, KNUST has reserved a quota for enrolments from deprived schools and regions, while the University of Ghana announced the designation of 300 admission slots for such students meeting the minimum entry requirements starting in 2004/2005. This suggests a growing recognition that students' access to university education is differentiated by socio-economic status and their schools of origin. Such criteria need to be adopted by all universities, since otherwise student pressure from those most vulnerable to exclusion could undermine the experiment by overloading the schools which comply. Correspondingly, a joint admissions and matriculations board, long recognized as a potential area of collaboration for publicly funded universities, may seem more feasible if universities can agree on these access and equity criteria.

152

Expanding access through the use of external degree centres and distance learning

External degree centres and distance-learning initiatives are under way and have been increasingly successful at the University of Ghana and UEW. These initiatives could be scaled up through inter-university co-operation and the use of ICT and library resources by opening up access and converting physical spaces for research, teaching and learning into virtual spaces. The University of Ghana, for example, owns 'Workers' College' facilities in every region of Ghana, which are under-utilized and under-funded. The UEW is also gradually establishing distance-learning centres in many regions of Ghana, while the UDS has a diverse structure of campuses in four of the country's ten regions. Scaling-up distance education and collaboration between universities through mutual credit systems could allow students to take accredited courses from multiple universities. Similarly, the External Degree Centre of the University of Ghana (now the Accra City Campus of the UG), which is in close proximity to the School of Languages, the Social Advance Institute and the Ghana Institute of Journalism, could form the basis for a city college for working people, lessening some of the pressures for admission into universities.

Deepening universities' relevance to societal needs

Teaching and research efforts that bring students and teachers into direct and ongoing engagement with societal needs, such as the third-trimester system practised in the University for Development Studies, have a real potential to position universities at the centre of socio-economic development and poverty reduction in Ghana, to reach the goal outlined in the conceptual framework. The emerging challenges of clean water and improved sanitation, as a remedy against ill health, disease and poverty in Africa call for a co-ordinated effort by scientific, socio-cultural and developmental disciplines to generate strategies and mobilize skills, investments and political commitment. Ghanaian universities can respond to such challenges through more proactive teaching, research and community services. Renewing linkages to indigenous knowledge is a crucial step towards reducing the extroversion of Ghanaian universities and making university knowledge production more rooted in and relevant for local communities. Only a conscious effort to

153

valorize indigenous written and oral knowledge and epistemologies, practices and educational strategies can ensure that the full range of Ghanaian human capabilities will be mobilized by higher education.

Universities as laboratories for innovation and change

As universities aspire to provide innovative solutions to societal problems, they should offer practical demonstrations of their potential. Using campuses as laboratories for new ideas would enhance students' practical training, as acquired skills in management, for instance, could be applied to university departments and facilities. Synergies can be created by making students and staff work creatively to confront problems such as waste management, environmental planning, job creation, the need for life-long learning and community integration. Considering that campuses are microcosms of society, they mirror larger problems while presenting an encapsulated environment that invites collective action by all inhabitants. By providing service-related job opportunities for students, campuses could serve as untapped sources of income for students and at the same time enable them to experience manual and cognitive labour in a complementary rather than hierarchical manner.

Applied research and industry linkages

The pioneering work undertaken by the Cocoa Processing Company and KNUST, as well as interactions between KNUST and the Kumasi *Suame* magazine, to work with largely illiterate mechanics and artisans who successfully produce spare parts for vehicles and fabricate machine tools, suggest the high potential for applied research and industry linkages.

University governance reforms and decentralization

The decentralization of governance systems, such as is under way at the UCC and being contemplated at the UDS and UEW, offers some important innovations in university management that nurture the nascent leadership potentials of faculty members. Individual staff are thereby enabled to assume risks, initiate change and take on new responsibilities within the university.

154

ICT as a catalyst for wider knowledge networks
Currently, ICT networks are either inter- or intra-university, bypassing and thus excluding industry and private users. But these networks could be transformed into knowledge networks with the potential of bringing academics into closer relations with practitioners in industry and government, and other virtual communities, such as school systems, districts and organized civil society institutions.

Strengthening libraries
Along with the introduction of ICTs as a catalyst for expanded information networks, libraries should be strengthened to allow universities to function as knowledge-production sites for staff, students and the public. For this to occur successfully, the following measures are needed: library funding should be direct and not dependent on the university, and librarians should be more involved in university governance. The libraries need to automate their catalogues to make them more accessible, with comprehensive training programmes for all library staff, particularly in the ICT area. To strengthen institutional collaboration, the CARLIGH interlibrary loan and document delivery network should be made viable. An intranet and a national bibliographic network-cum-database (OPAC) of the type provided for South Africa by the South African Bibliographic Information Network (SABINET) should be established, while CARLIGH should also mount a formal information literacy programme within the framework of its network of libraries. A representative from tertiary institutions is needed on the National Council for Distance Education.

Strengthening universities' engagement with public policy

There are minimal links between universities and the design of public policy. Possible linkages exist with ISSER at the University of Ghana, which produces authoritative information on the Ghanaian economy, and the new Centre for Education Policy at UEW, which offers evaluations of public educational policies. Such initiatives show the potential for universities to assist in shaping public policy. These should be strengthened and expanded. Connecting them to current public policy exercises such as the education policy review and the Ghana Poverty Reduction Strategy are a few of the possibilities.

155

Engagement and support for the government's poverty-reduction efforts

Each of the universities has a comparative advantage in areas of poverty reduction that could be brought to bear on the design, implementation, management and evaluation of poverty-reducing initiatives in Ghana. In turn, experiences gained through such engagements would feed back into the creation of new forms of knowledge, skills and the determination of the human resources of the society and economy to address poverty.

Building and strengthening strategic leadership

The growing use by universities of strategic planning tools for long-term change should include leadership at the three levels of faculty, staff and students. The Vice-Chancellors, Ghana (VCG) has an opportunity here to offer educational leadership, as a means of shaping policy and resource decisions by national policy-makers. The renaming of CVCP as Vice Chancellors, Ghana ought to redirect its mandate towards a more strategic leadership of the whole university system instead of focusing on discrete institutions and their concerns. VCG ought to explore opportunities for system-wide integration.

Meeting the demands of the future

In meeting future demands, some recommendations are offered to encourage more collaboration.

Collaborative graduate studies facilities

As the staff ages and new graduates do not return to their universities, a new approach is needed to support graduate training in Ghana. Such a programme must provide ample resources for graduates to study, complete with suitable accommodation and adequate research support. With local learning and research as the aim, opportunities for collaborative studies (at sister universities with compatible resources) should be encouraged.

Sharing resources for joint programming among universities

Inter- and intra–university collaboration through long-term departmental partnerships for course development and delivery should be

156

established, along with co-operative research projects and shared resources for graduate training. These synergies are exemplified by the relationship between the Department of Geography and Resource Development at the University of Ghana and the UCC Department of Geography and Tourism, and the growth of relationships between the three medical schools. There is also some co-ordination among the public universities, mostly initiated by individual personnel and departments. No explicit policies serve to encourage these sorts of arrangements, but many possibilities could be exploited. For example, the UG Institute of Adult Education has under-utilized facilities in each of the ten regional capitals, which could be used as distance-education resource centres for students from both public and private universities. The UEW also has a well-resourced centre for the development of study materials for distance-education programmes, which could be expanded to service other programmes as well.

There are additional opportunities for the collaborative use of resources within these institutions themselves. For instance, the resources of the African Virtual University, the Distance Education Centre and the Institute of Adult Education could be used to support the University of Ghana's distance and continuing education programmes. Some multi-disciplinary centres might help to foster such collaboration. The KNUST strategic plan describes such centres as a future development option.

Cooperation with private universities and new centres of knowledge creation

A challenge in need of attention from the public universities is the existence of new centres of knowledge creation as well as of private universities and their implications for human resource development and for the allocation of public resources to higher education. With current developments in ICT, universities could benefit greatly from high-speed global links connecting libraries. The possibilities for improved course development and delivery of course materials should benefit everyone through better resource utilization at a national level. These new centres could also contribute to staff training at the public universities in more cost-effective ways, as they also stand to benefit from improved staffing.

157

Managing change & transformation

For our recommendations to be realized, there is the need for conscious effort by each institution to build coalitions and innovative partnerships. Change-management teams should be established to review the strategic planning efforts at each university and to develop system-wide synergies for transformation in teaching, research and community services. Such teams could promote collaboration, share their experiences and encourage synergies in this process. Subsequently, a transformed VCG could co-ordinate cross-cutting university transformation activities.

The NCTE ought to play a proactive role in shaping a university process of policy evaluation and in lobbying for increased resources to facilitate this transformation.

Refocusing and making research a priority

The research capacity of staff and students should be a high priority for improvement through support and promotion and through the use of internal and external funding from industry and other sources. Institutional arrangements for monitoring and assessing research performance should be established as well. Opportunities for students to work with staff on projects and publications should be enhanced as a way of developing interest in new research.

Conclusion

This study represents the first structured attempt to combine qualitative and quantitative analyses of the state of public universities in Ghana. Despite the emergence of private universities and other centres of knowledge production and dissemination, the argument has been that public universities play an indispensable role in Ghanaian higher education and thus in national development. There is, however, the need to emphasize indigenous conceptions of education that valorize knowledge of traditions, technical skills and the ability to apply them to solving current problems to reconnect knowledge production in universities with the needs of surrounding communities, the country and the sub-region.

Rather than reducing education to a functionalist prerequisite of economic growth, an enhanced and holistic concept of development has been employed to reconceptualize education as a value in itself, a privilege that creates personal possibilities but also entails responsibility for the advancement of communal and societal well-being. There is the need therefore for a broader vision of the role of universities in Ghanaian society to foster the development of not just human capital, but human capabilities.

Universities should also attempt to provide spaces where experiences and perspectives that are under-valorized or marginalized in Ghanaian society can be expressed, so that tertiary institutions can learn to move beyond replicating societal exclusions based on gender or dis/ability towards really inclusive education.

Contrary to contemporary developmental discourse that pitches basic against higher education, the two are complementary and synergistic, similar to the relationship between universities and society at large. While universities face chronic under-funding, with negative effects on the human resource situation further complicated by the brain drain and increasing enrolments, there are also transformative initiatives that provide a blueprint for successful strategic planning and innovation. Identifying best practices and fostering co-operation and institutional learning are necessary steps towards enhancing the role of Ghana's public universities in an ongoing process towards a national endeavour encapsulated in the ambitious notion of 'development as freedom'.

159

Appendix
Institutional Profiles

Kwame Nkrumah University of Science & Technology

Kwame Nkrumah University of Science and Technology (KNUST) was established by a government ordinance in 1951 as the Kumasi College of Technology to provide higher education in science and technology, and to act as a catalyst for the technological development of the country. It opened officially on 22 January 1952, with 200 teacher training students transferred from Achimota College to form the nucleus of the new college. It attained university status in 1961 and started awarding degrees in June 1964.

Between 1951 and 1961, the college grew rapidly and underwent some major transformations. In October 1952, the School of Engineering and the Department of Commerce were established. A pharmacy department was established in January 1953, with the transfer of the former School of Pharmacy from Korle Bu Hospital, Accra, to the college. A Department of Agriculture was opened in the same year to provide a number of *ad hoc* courses of varying duration, from a few terms to three years, for what is now the Ministry of Food and Agriculture. A Department of General Studies was also instituted to prepare students for the Higher School Certificate Examinations in both science and arts subjects and to give instruction in such subjects as were requested by the other departments. In 1957, the School of Architecture, Town Planning and Building was established, and its first students were admitted in January 1958 for professional courses in architecture, town planning and building.

As the college expanded, it was decided to make the Kumasi College of Technology a pure science and technology institution. In pursuit of this policy, the Teacher Training College, with the exception of the Art School, was transferred in 1958 to the Winneba Training College (now the University of Education, Winneba), and in 1959 the Commerce Department was transferred to Achimota College to form the nucleus of the present School of Administration of the University of Ghana, Legon.

In 1961, following the report of the University Commission, which was appointed by the Government of Ghana to advise it on the future development of university education in the country, the government decided to establish two independent universities, one in Kumasi and the other at Legon near Accra. The Kumasi College of Technology was thus transformed into a fully-fledged university – Kwame Nkrumah University of Science and Technology – by an Act of Parliament on 22 August 1961. The name of the university was changed after the coup of February 1966 to the University of Science and Technology, Kumasi. The university reverted to its original name in 2000.

The university has two campuses on a total land area of 18.4 square km. The main campus is situated about 8 km away from the centre of Kumasi, the capital of Ashanti Region, and covers an area of about 18 square km. The second campus is at Tarkwa, and is now the Western University College (the former School of Mines, Tarkwa).

At the main campus, there are six halls of residence for students: three for both male and female students, two for male students only and one for female students only. There are also four hostels: one under the management of the Ghana Universities Staff Super-annuation Scheme (GUSSS) for both undergraduate and graduate students, two for postgraduate students and one at the Komfo Anokye Teaching Hospital for clinical medical students. The Social Security and National Insurance Trust (SSNIT) is constructing a fifth hostel.

The university has the following academic units:

- five faculties (Agriculture, Environmental & Development Studies, Pharmacy, Science and Social Sciences);
- two schools (Engineering and Medical Sciences);
- three institutes (Land Management & Development, Mining & Mineral Engineering and Renewable Natural Resources);
- one college (the College of Art);
- one university college (Western University College).

There are also a School of Graduate Studies, a Technology Consultancy Centre (TCC), a Centre for Cultural Studies (CCS), a Bureau of Integrated Rural Development (BIRD), the Kumasi Virtual Centre for Information Technology (KVCIT), the Centre for Distance Education (CDE) and the Institute of Technical Education (ITE).

The university also has a number of municipal facilities. These

161

include a hospital, basic schools (i.e. nursery, primary and junior secondary schools), a swimming pool, maintenance and estate organizations, a photocopying unit, a printing press, a bookshop, a senior staff club, a sports stadium, commercial and banking facilities, a post office and places of worship. A senior secondary school is also located on the Kumasi campus.

Graduates of the university are playing key roles in institutions such as the Volta River Authority (VRA), the Electricity Company of Ghana (ECG), the Ghana Water Company Limited (GWC) and the Cocoa Processing Company (CPC), where almost all the engineers are KNUST alumni. Similarly, the planners of the Town and Country Planning Department and the pharmacists of health institutions and retail pharmacies, as well as the engineers and architects at the forefront of activities in the design and construction sector, have been trained at KNUST. Based on the focus of the School of Medical Sciences and the steady growth of the Kumasi Centre for Collaborative Research in Tropical Medicine (KCCR), KNUST is making major contributions to meeting the human resource needs of Ghana's health sector.

With the involvement of the students in community service and outreach programmes and the re-tuning of the programmes to the manpower requirements of the national economy, the university is positioning itself to play an effective role and contribute meaningfully to both local and national socio-economic development.

Professional associations provide a bridge between industry and the university. Some of the professional associations and institutions are the Ghana Institution of Engineers, the Ghana Institute of Architects, the Ghana Institution of Surveyors, the Ghana Institute of Planners and the Ghana Science Association. Members of the professional associations serve as moderators for the academic programmes to make the contents more relevant to national needs, thus creating a ready market for their graduates.

University of Cape Coast

The vision of the University of Cape Coast is to be the university of choice in Ghana. Its mission is to provide comprehensive liberal and professional programmes that challenge learners to be creative and innovative. Established in 1962, it was mandated to train highly qualified and skilled human resources for the education sector, in response to the dire need for trained educators and administrators, especially for the Ghana Education Service and teachers for second-cycle institutions after the launching of the Accelerated Development Plan of 1959. It became an autonomous university in 1972. With time the university has expanded its original mandate and now offers programmes in tourism, business studies, population, environmental studies, computer science and laboratory technology.

In 2001/2, the student population numbered 9,822, of whom 27 per cent were females, while students in the Faculty of Education constituted 49 per cent of enrolments. Students in science-based programmes (B.Ed., Science, Agricultural Science, and Physical/Biological sciences) also accounted for about 20 per cent of the student population, far below the national target of a 60:40 ratio for science and humanities.

Currently, diploma and degree programmes are offered in four faculties and one school, namely, the School of Agriculture and the Faculties of Arts, Education, Science and Social Sciences. Within these four faculties and one school are 28 departments.

A number of institutes and centres have also been established in response to specific needs within the country and the university. These are:

i) The Institute of Education, which has oversight responsibility for all pre-university teacher education in Ghana. It is charged with the assessment and certification of all Teacher Training Colleges;
ii) The Institute for Educational Planning and Administration (IEPA), which trains high calibre practitioners in educational planning, administration and research. Its training programmes have been developed to satisfy the needs and requirements of the Ghana Education Service and the Ministry of Education, and include short in-service training courses; diploma (sandwich) courses; M.Phil/M.Ed/M.A programmes and M.Ed (sandwich) programmes;
iii) The Centre for Research on Improving the Quality of Primary Education in Ghana (CRIQPEG), set up in 1992 to carry out school/classroom-based research for the purpose of improving the quality of education at the primary school level. With support from USAID, the project seeks to develop processes

163

involved in integrating research into the classroom situation to improve the quality of teaching and learning in primary schools;

iv) The Centre for Continuing Education, formerly known as the Centre for Distance Education, was established in 1997. Its focus is to provide teacher education programmes through distance learning. The first phase of the programme targets basic school teachers and leads to the award of a Diploma in Basic Education;

v) The Counselling Centre offers counselling services to students, staff of the university and the general public;

vi) The Laser and Fibre Optics Centre (LAFOC) was set up with the help of the Abdus Salam International Centre for Theoretical Physics (Italy). It aims at training scientists, technicians and engineers in modern optical design, and is located in the Department of Physics. The Centre had graduated three doctoral students as of the end of the 2001/2 academic year, two of whom are currently teaching at the Department of Physics.

vii) The Centre for Development Studies was established to undertake research on issues of socio-economic development and to participate in national and international efforts to identify and understand the processes and mechanisms of development, and contribute to the stock of information needed by policy-makers and administrators to solve development problems. The Centre also runs inter-disciplinary M.Phil. and Ph.D degrees in Development Studies.

viii) The African Virtual University UCC Site was launched in March 1998, and offers programmes for technicians, engineers, healthcare providers and other professionals.

The university has a 2,000-seating capacity library with about 600,000 books and 500 titles of journals/periodicals. The library complex, started in 1977, was completed in 1998 and has facilities for e-mail, Internet and inter-library Loan and Document Delivery. A continuing challenge is stocking the library to meet the growing needs of students and faculty.

University of Education of Winneba (UEW)

The University College of Education was established by the government in 1992. The college came into existence through the amalgamation of what were formerly known as the Specialist

Training College (STC), the National Academy of Music (NAM) and the Advanced Teachers Training College (ATTC), all located at Winneba; the School of Ghana Languages, Ajumako; the College of Special Education, Mampong-Akwapim; St Andrews Agricultural Training College, Mampong-Ashanti; and the Kumasi Advanced Technical Teachers College (KATTC), Kumasi. It became University College of Education, Winneba in 2005.

It has 7,631 students and is the largest teacher education university in Ghana. It has earned a worldwide reputation as a centre of excellence. UCEW has three campuses, with the main campus at Winneba, a town in the Central Region of Ghana 66 km west of Accra, and satellite campuses in Kumasi and Mampong-Ashanti.

The UEW runs the following programmes:

- a three-year enhanced Diploma
- a one-year full-time post-diploma B.Ed.
- a one-year sandwich post-diploma B.Ed., and
- a four-year B.Ed.

The university has excellent links with major international and national agencies, non-governmental organizations, ministries of education and universities throughout the world.

The UEW's mission is to develop the university to serve as a centre of excellence based on academic proficiency, professional competence and humanistic values for teaching and on the production of instructional materials in addition to the dissemination of relevant knowledge at the basic level of education and teacher training colleges.

The UEW provides a wide range of full-time, sandwich and distance-education programmes. The university college has five divisions and one institute, all operating at the faculty level. The five divisions comprise 15 academic departments and two units. The Institute for Educational Development and Extension (IEDE) is organized into five units. Two centres – the Basic Education Centre and the Educational Resource Centre – also aid academic work.

The University for Development Studies

The University for Development Studies was established in 1992 as a multi-campus institution with its headquarters at Tamale. It was

165

envisaged to have campuses located in the four administrative regions that comprise the northern sector of Ghana (Brong-Ahafo, Northern, Upper East and Upper West Regions). Although not all the campuses are yet operational, campuses are to be located at Tamale, Nyankpala, Navrongo, Kintampo and Wa. The university currently has a student population of about 1,000 students.

Unlike the older universities in Ghana, the law establishing the University for Development Studies vested it from its inception with the power to award its own degrees, diplomas, certificates, honorary degrees and other academic distinctions. Among other aims, the founders envisaged that the university would provide higher education that would 'blend the academic world with that of the community in order to provide constructive interaction between the two for the total development of northern Ghana in particular and Ghana as a whole.'

It was further envisaged that the university would attract a new breed of students who would not only be practically oriented and community-based but would also be made 'aware of their responsibility to use their education for the general good of the Ghanaian society'. The mandate encouraged practical studies without sacrificing academic excellence. It was expected that, working with local resources, students would gain an appreciation of and concern for community perceptions and aspirations that would keep them in rural areas and address the brain-drain issue as well.

The university's aims, mission and mandate emphasize the social sciences as vehicles for addressing the varied development issues prevailing in the north of the country, and, by extension, downplay the relevance of the arts in addressing contemporary development issues.

The university currently has four faculties, one centre and departments as indicated below:

Agriculture – six departments
Applied Sciences – four departments
Integrated Development Studies – five departments
School of Medicine & Health Sciences
Centre for Inter-Disciplinary Research.

University of Ghana

The University of Ghana was founded in 1948 as the University College of the Gold Coast, on the recommendation of the Asquith Commission of Higher Education for the purpose of providing and promoting university education, learning, and research in the then British colony. At its inception, the college enjoyed a special relationship with the University of London whereby it was allowed to teach for the latter's external degree examinations. By an act of Parliament in 1961, the college attained full university status with authority to award its own degrees and diplomas.

The university is located 15 km northeast of Accra on Legon Hill some 450 feet above sea level. Apart from the College of Health Sciences and three of its constituent colleges, which are located in Korle Bu, the External Degree Centre of the Institute of Adult Education in central Accra, and the Agricultural Research Stations in other parts of the country, all other faculties, departments and institutes of the university are located at the main campus.

The university has a well-planned infrastructure comprising halls of residence and departmental buildings occupying the central portions of the main campus. Residential buildings housing some of the teaching and non-teaching staff form part of this infrastructure and provide an atmosphere where staff and students can interact outside of the lecture and laboratory periods.

The infrastructure of the university comprising the academic and residential buildings has changed little since the university was established. Teaching facilities are generally inadequate, but in recent years, through support from the government and international donor agencies, the university has been able to add new structures. Notable among these are the Common Lecture Theatre Complex and the chemistry building. Currently under construction are office and lecture rooms for the Institute of African Studies, the Faculty of Law and the Legon Centre for International Affairs.

Residential accommodation for students started with five grouped halls of residence: Legon Hall (mixed), Akuafo Hall (mixed), Mensah Sarbah Hall (mixed), Commonwealth Hall (male) and Volta Hall (female). These are inadequate for the large numbers of students, and there is overcrowding and stress on facilities in these halls. Four hostels have been added to the above-mentioned traditional halls of residence in past years: these are Annexe C of Legon Hall, the Valco

167

Trust Hostel, the International Student Hostel and Jubilee Hall.

Recognizing the financial limitations on the construction of new residential facilities for students, the university has entered into partnerships with private developers to build hostels on the campus. The first privately owned hostel was constructed by the Social Security and National Insurance Trust (SSNIT) and was opened for students for the 2001/2 academic year. This hostel has had very high patronage.

The current student population of the university is 15,991, made up of 10,494 (64.6 per cent) males and 5,494 (34.4 per cent) females. The foreign student population is 238 (2 per cent of the total student population). The staff population currently stands at 4,086, of which 3,229 (79 per cent) are male and 857 (21 per cent) female. Senior members, senior staff and junior staff constitute 17.3 per cent, 24 per cent and 58.8 per cent of the staff population, respectively (University of Ghana, 2002a).

Academic life in the university is centred around a college, six faculties, two schools, six institutes, each of which is attached to a faculty or college, and nine centres of research and learning as indicated below:

- The College of Health Sciences: Comprises four schools, one research institute and a Department, namely, the Medical and Dental Schools, the School of Allied Health Sciences, the School of Public Health, the Noguchi Memorial Institute for Medical Research and the Nursing Department.
- Faculty of Agriculture: Agricultural Economy/Farm Management, Agricultural Engineering; Soil Science; Crop Science; Agricultural Extension; Home Science.
- Faculty of Law: (non-departmentalized). Offers post-first degree programmes only.
- Faculty of Arts: Classics, English, Language Centre, Linguistics, Modern Languages (Arabic, French, Russian, Spanish and Swahili), Philosophy, Study of Religions and the School of Performing Arts (with Departments of Dance Studies, Music and Theatre Arts).
- Faculty of Science: Biochemistry, Botany, Chemistry, Computer Science, Fisheries & Oceanography, Geology, Mathematics, Nursing, Nutrition & Food Science, Psychology, Physics, Statistics and Zoology.

168

- Faculty of Social Studies: Archaeology, Economics, Geography & Resource Development, History, Information Studies, Mathematics, Nursing, Political Science, Psychology, Sociology & Social Work, School of Performing Arts and School of Communication Studies.
- School of Administration: The school, which has the status of a faculty, comprises five academic units as follows: Accounting, Management (Finance & Banking, Insurance, Marketing, Human Resources), Health Services, Administration, Public Administration and Management Information Systems (MIS).

The institutes are the Institute of African Studies, the Institute of Adult Education, the Institute of Statistical, Social & Economic Research (ISSER), Noguchi Memorial Institute for Medical Research (NMIMR), Regional Institute of Population Studies (RIPS) and the United Nations Institute for National Resources of Africa (INRA).

The centres include the External Degree Centre, the Regional Training Centre for Archivists (formerly the Department of Library & Archival Studies), the Language Centre, the Legon Centre for International Affairs (LECIA), the Centre for Tropical Clinical Pharmacology & Therapeutics, the International Centre for African Music & Dance, the Ecology Laboratory Centre, the Centre for Social Policy Studies and the Consultancy Centre.

Other research units and faculties include the Volta Basin Research Project (VBRP), the Legon Seismological Observatory, the Legon Botanical Gardens, the Agricultural Research Station (comprising the Nungua, Kpong and Kade Stations), the Remote Sensing and Applications Unit and the African Virtual University.

169

References

Abegaz, Berhanu M. and Lisbeth A. Levey. 1996. *What Price Information? Priority Setting in African Universities*. Washington, DC: American Association for the Advancement of Science.

Addae-Mensah, Ivan. 2000. 'Education in Ghana: A Tool for Social Mobility or Social Stratification?' Delivered at J. B. Danquah Memorial Lectures, Ghana Academy of Arts and Sciences, Accra.

———. 2001. 'Matriculation Address', in 'Proceedings of the Matriculation of the University of Ghana', *University of Ghana Special Reporter* No. 699, 40, 4.

Adu, K. and K.J. Opoku-Afriyie. 2002. *Expenditure and Revenue Analysis of Tertiary Institutions in Ghana, 1996-2000*. Accra: Ministry of Education.

African Gender Institute. 2002. 'Strengthening Gender and Women's Studies in African Contexts'. http://www.gwsafrica.org/search/index.html [accessed 15 January 2006].

Agbodeka, F. 1998. *A History of University of Ghana: Half a Century of Higher Education (1948–1998)*. Accra: Woeli Publishing Services.

Ajayi, J.F. Ade, Lameck K.H. Goma and G. Ampah Johnson. 1996. *The African Experience with Higher Education*. Association of African Universities. Oxford: James Currey and Athens, OH: Ohio University Press.

Akyeampong, D.A. et al. 1998. 'Education in Ghana'. Unpublished report, University Planning Unit, Legon.

Albrecht, D. and A. Ziderman. 1991. *Referred Cost Recovery for Higher Education: Students Loan Programs in Developing Countries*. World Bank Discussion Paper. Washington, DC: World Bank.

Assie-Lumumba, N.T. 1995. 'Demand, Access and Equity Issues in African Higher Education'. Background Paper for the Joint Colloquium on the University in Africa in the 1990s and Beyond, Association of African Universities, Accra.

———. 2001. 'Gender, Race and Human Capital Theory: Research Trends', in special issue on the United States from the 1950s to the 1990s. *Journal of Comparative Education and International Relations in Africa* 4, 1: 1–25.

Association of African Universities. 1991. *Study on Cost Effectiveness and Efficiency in African Universities: A Synthesis Report*. Accra: AAU.

Badat, S. 2002. 'Transforming South African Higher Education, 1990–2000: Context, Goals, Policy Processes and Key Challenges'. African Higher Education Partnership Meeting, Abuja, Nigeria.

Badu, E. E. 1998. 'Towards an Information Provision Strategy for University Libraries in Ghana: The Relevance of Recent Developments in the United Kingdom'. Ph.D. thesis, University of Sheffield.

Batse, Z. M. K. and O. Gyekye. 1992. *Graduate Tracer Study: A Study of Employed and Unemployed Graduates in Ghana*. Report to the Ministry of Education Higher Education Division. Accra.

Becker, G. S. 1964. *Human Capital.* New York: National Bureau of Economic Research.

Bennett, J. 2002. 'Exploration of a "Gap": Strategising Gender Equity in African Universities,' *Feminist Africa* 1: 34–65.

Black, R., K. Russell and R. Tiemoko. 2003. *Migration, Return and Small Enterprise Development in Ghana: a route out of poverty?* Sussex Migration Working Paper no 9. Brighton: Sussex Migration Research Centre. http://www.sussex.ac.uk/USIS/test/migration/documents/mwp9.pdf [accessed 15 January 2006].

Budu, J. M. 1998. *A Profile of Ghanaian Universities.* Report compiled for Association of Commonwealth Universities.

Budu, J. M., V. Acheampong and A. Quartey. 2002. 'Report on Study on ICT Management and Use in Selected Universities in Ghana'. Unpublished report undertaken as part of the Ghana Universities Case Study. Accra.

California State University, Northridge (CSUN). 1997. 'Strategic Plan Document'.

Centre for Economic Policy Analysis (CEPA). 2000. *Macroeconomic Revi* *and Outlook.* Accra: CEPA.

Daily Graphic. Various issues, 2001–3.

Dakubu, M. and B. Adomako-Owusu. 2002. *Information Communica ns Technology Development Strategy Plan in the Tertiary Education Sect in Ghana.* Accra: National Council for Tertiary Education (NCTE).

De Bruijn, D. and K. Robertson. 1997. 'Beyond Collections to Conne ns: Increasing Library Capacity in Ghana'. Prepared for the Common alth of Learning, with support from the UK Overseas Development A inistration.

Effah, P. 2003. 'Ghana', in Damtew Teferra and Philip G. Altba (eds), *African Higher Education: An International Reference Handbook.* B omington, IN: Indiana University Press.

Effah, P. and H. J. A. N. Mensah-Bonsu. 2001. *Governance of Terti / Education Institutions in Ghana: A Manual.* Accra: NCTE.

Ekong, D. and P. Plante. 1996. *Strategic Planning at Selected Afr 1 Universities.* Accra: Association of African Universities.

Fakinlede, O. 2001. 'Case Study of ICT at Nigerian Universities'. Prepared for Information and Communications Technology Component Project. Partnership for Higher Education in Africa.

Garbe, A. 2004. 'Networking among Senior Members at the University of Ghana'. Unpublished M.Phil thesis submitted to the University of Ghana, Legon.

Ghana Academy of Arts and Sciences. 1981. *Handbook.* Accra: Ghana Publishing Corporation.

Ghana Education Service. 2002. *Cost of Education per Child, Pre-Tertiary Level.* Accra: GES.

Girdwood, A. 1999. *Tertiary Education Policy in Ghana: An Assessment: 1988– 1998.* Washington, DC: World Bank.

Gyekye, Kwame. 2002. *A Vision for Post-Graduate Education in Ghana.* NCTE

171

Technical Report Series. Accra: NCTE.

Hountondji, P. J. 2003. 'Knowledge Appropriation in a Post-Colonial Context', in C.A.O. Hoppers (ed.), *Indigenous Knowledge and the Integration of Knowledge Systems: Towards a Philosophy of Articulation.* Johannesburg and Cape Town: New Africa Books.

Hutchful, E. 2002. *Ghana's Adjustment Experience – The Paradox of Reform.* Oxford: James Currey and Accra: Woeli Publishing Services in association with UNRISD, Geneva.

Kennedy, P. 1993. *Preparing for the Twenty-First Century.* New York: Random House.

Killick, T. 1978. *Development Economics in Action: A Study of Economic Policies in Ghana.* London: Heinemann.

Kisiedu, C. O. 2002. 'Ghana Universities Case Study: Study on Libraries in the Public Universities in Ghana'. Unpublished manuscript prepared as part of the Ghana Universities Case Study.

Kwame Nkrumah University of Science and Technology. 2001. *PLAN2K10. [Strategic Plan 2001–2010].* Kumasi: KNUST.

——. 2002a. *Institutional Profile.* Prepared by S. Owusu and N.B. Adomako, Counterpart Team members, Kumasi.

——. 2002b. '2002 Budget'. Kumasi.

——. 2004. 'Socio-Economic Background of Students in Tertiary Institutions'. Technology Consultancy Centre. Unpublished draft report.

Kwesiga, J. 2002. *Women's Access to Higher Education in Africa: Uganda's Experience.* Kampala: Fountain Publishers.

Lerner, A.L. 1999. 'Strategic Planning Essays'. Unpublished manuscript. Northridge, CA: California State University.

Mama, A. 2002. 'Intellectual Politics', editorial, *Feminist Africa* 1: 1–8.

——. 2003. 'Gender Studies for Africa's Transformation'. Paper Presented at CODESRIA 30th Anniversary Grand Finale, Dakar.

Mamdani, M. 2002. 'African Universities in their Local and Global Contexts'. Paper presented at Partnership for Higher Education Workshop. Abuja, Nigeria, 18 March.

Manuh, T. 1998. *Women in Africa's Development: Overcoming Obstacles, Pushing for Progress.* Africa Recovery Briefing Paper. New York: United Nations Department of Public Information.

Mkandawire, T. 2001. 'Social Policy in a Development Context'. UNRISD Society, Policy & Development Programme, Paper No. 7. Geneva: UNRISD. Available at www.unrisd.org/publications [accessed 14 September 2006]

—— and C. C. Soludo. 1999. *Our Continent, Our Future.* Dakar: Council for the Development of Social Science Research in Africa and International Development Research Center.

MOE/GES. 2002. Ministry of Education Ghana Education Service. GES, Administration and Finance Division, cited in Republic of Ghana (2002a).

NCTE. 1998. *Evaluation of the Policy Objectives of the Reforms to the Tertiary Education System.* NCTE Technical Report Series 2. Accra: NCTE.

——. 1999. *Handbook.* Accra: NCTE.

——. 2002. *Annual Report.* Accra: NCTE.

——. 2004. *Statistics on Public Tertiary Education Institutions.* Accra: NCTE.

Ng'ethe, Njuguna, N'dri Assié-Lumumba, George Subotzky and Esi Sutherland-Addy, 2003. *Regional Survey of Innovations in Higher Education: Synthesis Report.* ADEA Working Group on Higher Education. Accra: Association of African Universities.

Palmer, I. 1991. *Gender and Population in the Adjustment of African Economics: Planning for Change.* Geneva: International Labour Organization.

Pereira, C. 2002. 'Between Knowing and Imagining: What Space for Feminism in Scholarship on Africa?' *Feminist Africa* 1: 9–33.

Private Enterprise Foundation (PEF). 1997. 'Report on National Forum on Funding of Tertiary Education', held at Akosombo 27–28 January. Accra.

Prah, Mensah, 2002. 'Chasing Illusions and Realising Visions: Reflections on Ghana's Feminist Experience', Paper presented to CODESRIA conference, 'Intellectuals, Nationalism and the Pan-African Ideal.' 10–12 December. Dakar.

—— and A. A. Ampofo. (in preparation). 'Punishment, Discipline and Violence Against Women and Children in Ghana'.

Republic of Ghana. 1991. *Government White Paper on the Reforms to the Tertiary Education System.* Accra: Government Printe.

——. 1995. *Ghana-Vision 2020 (The First Step, 1996–2000).* Accra: Government Printer.

——. 2001. *National Draft IT Policy Plan.* Accra: Government Printer.

——. 2002a. *Meeting the Challenges of Education in the Twenty-First Century. Report of the President's Committee on Review of Education Reforms in Ghana.* Accra: Government Printer.

——. 2002b. 'Economic Policy Framework'. Vol. 1. Paper prepared by the mini-CG Secretariat for the Eleventh Meeting of the Consultative Group for Ghana, Accra: Government Printer.

——. 2003a. *An Agenda for Growth and Prosperity. Ghana Poverty Reduction Strategy 2003–2005. Vol. I: Analysis and Policy Statement.* Accra: Government Printer.

——. 2003b. *The Ghana ICT for Accelerated Development (CTAD) Policy.* Accra: Government Printer.

——. Ministry of Education. 1995. *Report on Study on Income Generation in Tertiary Education.* Prepared by Kingsley Adu et al. Accra: Government Printer.

——. 2001. *Policies and Strategic Plans for the Education Sector.* Accra: Government Printer.

——. Statistical Service. 2000. *Poverty Trends in the 1990s.* Accra: Government Printer.

Rowley, D. J. et al. 1997. *Strategic Change in Colleges and Universities.* San Francisco: Jossey-Bass Publishers.

Saint, W. S. 1992. *Universities in Africa: Strategies for Stabilization and Revitalization.* World Bank Technical Paper No. 194, Africa Technical

173

Department Series. Washington, DC: World Bank.

Sall, E. (ed.) 2000. *Women in Academia: Gender and Academic Freedom in Africa.* The State of Academic Freedom in Africa Series. Dakar: CODESRIA.

Sall, E., Y. Lebeau and R. Kassimir. 2003. 'The Public Dimensions of the University in Africa', *Journal of Higher Education in Africa* 1,1: 126–48.

Structural Adjustment Participatory Review Initiative (SAPRI). 2001. 'Structural Adjustment and Tertiary Education in Ghana (1983–99)'. Presented at Second National SAPRI Forum, Accra.

Sawyerr, A. 1994. 'Ghana: Relations Between Government and Universities', in G. Neave and F. V. Vught (eds), *Government and Higher Education Relationships Across Three Countries: The Winds of Change.* Oxford: Pergamon Press.

——. 2002. 'Challenges Facing African Universities – Selected Issues'. *Newsletter of the Social Science Academy of Nigeria* 5, 1: 25–30.

Sen, A. 1999. *Development as Freedom.* Oxford and New York: Oxford University Press.

Schultz, T. W. 1961. 'Investment in Human Capital', in Jerome Karabel and A. H. Halsey (eds), *Power and Ideology in Education.* New York: Oxford University Press.

Snesdon, J. 1998. 'Report on the Implementation of the Ghana Higher Education Management Information System'. Unpublished manuscript.

Szerezewski, R. 1965. *Structural Changes in the Economy of Ghana, 1891–1911.* London: Weidenfield and Nicolson.

Tsikata, D. (ed.) 2001. *Gender Training in Ghana: Politics, Issues and Tools.* Accra: Woeli Publishing Services.

University of Cape Coast. 2000. *Strategic Plan.* Cape Coast: University of Cape Coast.

——. 2002a. *Institutional Profile.* Prepared by I. Ohene and K. Awusabo-Asare, Counterpart Team Members. Cape Coast.

——. 2002b. *Thirty-second Congregation – Basic Statistics.* Cape Coast: University of Cape Coast.

University of Development Studies. 2002. *Institutional Profile.* Prepared by F.Z.L. Bacho and S.M. Kuu-ire, Counterpart Team Members. Tamale.

University College of Education, Winneba. 2002. *Institutional Profile.* Prepared by C. Y. Mensah and Kofi Mereku, Counterpart Team Members. Winneba.

University of Ghana. 1992. 'Strategic Plan 1992–2000'. Legon, University of Ghana.

——. 1995. 'A Study on the Socio-Economic Background of Students in Tertiary Institutions in Ghana'. Unpublished manuscript, Planning Unit.

——. 2001. *Corporate Strategic Plan.* Legon. University of Ghana.

——. 2002a. *Basic Statistics.* Legon. University of Ghana.

——. 2002b. *Financial Statements.* Legon. University of Ghana.

——. 2002c. 'Report of the Provost'. First Congregation of the College of Health Sciences, University of Ghana, May 25. Legon.

——. 2002d. *Institutional Profile.* Prepared by S. Sefa-Dede & Ama Kwaa,

Counterpart Team members.

——. 2004. *Basic Statistics.* Legon. University of Ghana.

UNESCO. 1998. *Benchmarking in Higher Education.* New papers on Higher Education Series 21. Paris: UNESCO

World Bank. 2000. *Higher Education in Developing Countries: Peril and Promise.* Washington, DC: World Bank.

——. 2003. *Evaluation of the CDF. Ghana Case Study.* Accra: World Bank, June.

Yankah, K. 1995. *Speaking for the Chief: Okyeame and the Politics of Akan Royal Oratory.* Bloomington, IN: Indiana University Press.

Yeboah, F. K. (ed). 1994. 'Effective Management of Resources in Higher Education Institutions'. *Report of Proceedings of a Seminar on Higher Education Administration in Ghana.* Accra: Committee of Vice Chancellors and Principals.

Zeleza, P.T. 2003 *Rethinking Africa's Globalization. Volume 1: The Intellectual Challenges.* Trenton, NJ: Africa World Press.

175